25

STEPPENWOLF

STEPPENWOLF THEATRE COMPANY
Twenty-five Years of an Actor's Theater

PORTRAITS BY
VICTOR SKREBNESKI

REFLECTIONS BY
Richard Christiansen   Don DeLillo   Sam Shepard   Kurt Vonnegut   Terry Johnson   Charles L. Mee

PRODUCTION PHOTOGRAPHY BY
Michael Brosilow   Lisa Ebright   Kevin Rigdon

SOURCEBOOKS, INC.
NAPERVILLE, ILLINOIS

CO-FOUNDERS: JEFF PERRY TERRY KINNEY GARY SINISE

HISTORY

Under the leadership of high school and college friends Gary Sinise, Terry Kinney and Jeff Perry, the Steppenwolf Theatre Company began performing plays informally in 1974 at various locations in Highland Park, Illinois, a suburb of Chicago. In 1975, the three co-founders incorporated the theater and, in 1976, expanded the group to include fellow Illinois State University friends H. E. Baccus, Nancy Evans, Moira Harris, John Malkovich, Laurie Metcalf and Alan Wilder. That summer, this ensemble of actors officially inaugurated the Steppenwolf Theatre Company by presenting a series of one–act plays in their first theater home in a church school basement in Highland Park. These one-acts included Israel Horovitz's *The Indian Wants the Bronx*, Leonard Melfi's *Birdbath*, Eugene Ionesco's *The Lesson* and Harold Pinter's *The Lover*. Inspired by positive early reviews and a growing public interest in the theatrical endeavors of the young company, Steppenwolf moved in 1980 into its first Chicago home, a 134-seat theater at the Jane Addams Hull House Center at 3212 North Broadway Avenue. Some of the company's early successes presented here included Lanford Wilson's *Balm in Gilead*, John Steinbeck's *Of Mice and Men* and Sam Shepard's *True West*. By now, the acting ensemble had grown to include Joan Allen, Francis Guinan, Glenne Headly, Tom Irwin, John Mahoney and Rondi Reed. As the company continued to grow artistically, and the demand for seats increased, Steppenwolf moved again in 1982, to a 211-seat facility at 2851 North Halsted Street in Chicago. It was at this location that Steppenwolf began to receive sustained national attention with productions such as C.P. Taylor's *And a Nightingale Sang...*,

John DiFusco's *Tracers,* Lyle Kessler's *Orphans* and Lynn Siefert's *Coyote Ugly* and *Little Egypt.* In 1985, the company received the Tony Award for Regional Theatre Excellence. The ensemble grew to include Kevin Anderson, Randall Arney, Robert Breuler, Gary Cole, Frank Galati, Tim Hopper, Austin Pendleton, Molly Regan, Rick Snyder and Jim True. During this period the company embarked on the development of one of its most ambitious projects— ensemble member Frank Galati's adaptation and direction of John Steinbeck's Pulitzer Prize-winning novel *The Grapes of Wrath.* After months of workshops, rehearsals and performances in Chicago, La Jolla and London, Steppenwolf opened *The Grapes of Wrath* on Broadway in the spring of 1990 and won the Tony Award for Best Play and Best Director. Once again, the company outgrew its theater and in April of 1991, Steppenwolf moved to its permanent home

Ensemble 1976

at 1650 North Halsted Street in Chicago. The state-of-the-art facility, owned and operated by the company, has a 510-seat Broadway-style Mainstage auditorium, a 200-seat Studio Theatre, a 60-seat Garage Theatre, rehearsal halls and administrative offices. Ensemble expansion has included the addition of Kathryn Erbe, K. Todd Freeman, Tina Landau, Martha Lavey, Mariann Mayberry, Amy Morton, Sally Murphy, Martha Plimpton, Eric Simonson and Lois Smith.

Propelled by the desire for distinctive artistic challenges, the ensemble works with playwrights, directors and designers to produce existing plays, as well as world premieres. Significant Mainstage productions have included Tug Yourgrau's *The Song of Jacob Zulu,* Don DeLillo's *Libra,* Anthony Burgess' *A Clockwork Orange,* William Faulkner's *As I Lay Dying,* Sam Shepard's *Buried Child,* Stephen

Jeffreys' *The Libertine,* Kurt Vonnegut's *Slaughterhouse-5,* Tina Landau's *Space,* Charles L. Mee's *The Berlin Circle,* Terry Johnson's *Hysteria* and Dale Wasserman's *One Flew Over the Cuckoo's Nest.* Successful Chicago productions have led to numerous New York productions. In 1982, the company made its New York debut with *True West* at the Cherry Lane Theatre. Since then, Steppenwolf has transferred to New York *And a Nightingale Sang…, Balm in Gilead, Orphans, The Caretaker, Educating Rita, The Grapes of Wrath, The Song of Jacob Zulu, The Rise and Fall of Little Voice* and, most recently, the Broadway production of *Buried Child,* which garnered five 1996 Tony Award nominations. Steppenwolf's reputation for ground-breaking, innovative theater infused with superior acting has also sparked world interest.

Ensemble 1980 *Photograph: Lisa Ebright*

In 1986, *Orphans* moved from New York to London's Hampstead Theatre and again to the Apollo Theatre in London's West End. In 1987, Steppenwolf brought *Lydie Breeze* to the Festivals of Sydney and Perth, Australia. In 1992, *A Slip of the Tongue* opened in London's West End. In 1993, *The Song of Jacob Zulu* was featured at the Festival of Perth, Australia. *The Man Who Came to Dinner* was part of the Barbican Centre's *Inventing America* festival in London in 1998. Steppenwolf returned to the Barbican in 2000 with their production of *One Flew Over the Cuckoo's Nest.* In addition, the company's production of the Tony Award-winning play *Side Man* was part of the 2000 International Arts Festival of Galway, marking the first time the work of the ensemble had been seen in Ireland.

The company's first Steppenwolf Studio Theatre transfer was Steve Martin's *Picasso at the Lapin Agile,* which opened in 1994 at the Westwood Playhouse in Los Angeles, and has since played successfully in numerous cities in the U.S. and abroad. *Picasso at the Lapin Agile* inaugurated the Steppenwolf Studio Theatre with its world premiere production in October of 1993. Recognizing the strengths of the company's first intimate home in Highland Park, Steppenwolf transformed a rehearsal space on the first floor of its parking garage building in May 1998 into a 60-seat theater. Called The Garage at Steppenwolf, the theater offers work on a smaller scale, as well as the opportunity to produce new work. The space was inaugurated with the American premiere of Hilary Bell's *Wolf Lullaby.* In November 1998, Steppenwolf became the first theater troupe ever awarded the National Medal of Arts, which was presented to the ensemble by President Bill Clinton and First Lady Hillary Rodham Clinton in a White House ceremony. The Medal honors individuals and organizations "who in the President's judgment are deserving of special recognition by reason of their outstanding contributions to the excellence, growth, support and availability of the arts in the United States."

Ensemble 1998 *Photograph: Carol Powers*

After twenty-five years as a professional theater, Steppenwolf Theatre Company has received national and international recognition from media, theater critics and audiences alike. Based on a commitment to the principles of ensemble collaboration and artistic risk, the mission of Steppenwolf is to advance the vitality and diversity of American theater, while maintaining the original, ensemble-based impulses of the group.

RICHARD CHRISTIANSEN

Richard Christiansen is senior writer and chief critic for the Chicago Tribune. In 1976, as critic-at-large for the Chicago Daily News, he attended and reviewed Steppenwolf Theatre Company's first summer of one-act productions. Mr. Christiansen, a seven-time member and twice chairman of the Pulitzer Prize drama jury, has attended and reviewed nearly every Steppenwolf production since.

"And It All Happened in the Theater"

It was up the hill, off Deerfield Road in Highland Park, and it was indeed in the basement. Above the church school building, there was a grassy plot that served as a parking lot, hard to navigate in wintry weather. In spring, on a mild evening, if you took an intermission stroll outside, you could see the actors pacing and smoking in one of the upstairs classrooms. Inside, there were sixty, maybe seventy, seats which lined three sides of the open rectangular stage. Like most small theaters in the Chicago area in that remarkably creative period of the mid-'70s, Steppenwolf was makeshift, homemade, youthful and talented. What distinguished it, above all, was that, right or wrongheaded, every production seemed new, freshly minted, double-daring in intensity, feverishly in the moment. In the audience, you were right in the middle of it.

Sometimes, this was dangerous. When Gary Sinise and Terry Kinney came roaring onto the stage as the two violent street punks of *The Indian Wants the Bronx* (I found out later that, to make their entrance, they went outside, ran down the hill at breakneck speed and then burst into the theater), I truly feared that, after terrorizing that lost and helpless Indian in Israel Horovitz's play, they were going to turn around and come after me.

Those early shows were great mines of discovery, bits and pieces of which I can never forget. There was *The Glass Menagerie,* in a production directed by H.E. Baccus (who later left the company, alas) that boldly shook up the play, taking it out of its customary wistful mode. John Malkovich played Tom, the son (and narrator) of Tennessee Williams' memory play, as openly gay, and Laurie Metcalf triumphantly went against the usual portrayal of his sister Laura as a fragile flower by playing her as a clumping cripple who was clearly headed for a mental institution.

There were marvelous disasters, too. Bowing to the request of board members who wanted a little relief from such heavy-duty depression, the company put on a musical revue. A great concept, except no one in the troupe, aside from Jeff Perry, could carry a tune. (To this day, whenever I hear "Speak Low," it is Jeff I see, standing in an aisle of the tiny theater and crooning that tune.)

Once they moved into Chicago, there were more discoveries: John Mahoney's breakthrough performance as the gangster/father figure of Lyle Kessler's *Orphans;* Joan Allen's luminous presence in the sweet English drama *And a Nightingale Sang...;* Laurie's incredible monologue in *Balm in Gilead,* made all the more absorbing by the total commitment with which Glenne Headly listened to it; Jeff (and later Gary) tearing up the stage with John Malkovich as the brawling siblings in the classic Steppenwolf high-energy performance

The Glass Menagerie 1979 Photograph: Lisa Ebright

of Sam Shepard's *True West;* and, out of the attic of my memory, yet still indelible, Moira Harris, in black leather, strutting about with a whip in hand in a late-show comic extravaganza that had something to do with (I think) a battling Mommy and Daddy.

Years later, in Tina Landau's buoyant staging of Charles L. Mee's *The Berlin Circle* in the big new theater at 1650 North Halsted Street, Amy Morton, portraying a wealthy American woman whose wild adventures had started when she attended a play, stepped to the front of the stage, and, speaking of the awesome events she had experienced, said, with beguiling innocence, "And to think it all happened in the theater." I laughed, and then, suddenly, the line having triggered a flood of my own memories of attending and reviewing plays at Steppenwolf, I was overwhelmed with emotion. Yes, over the years, it had happened in the theater. And, wonderful, I had been there to see it.

AMY MORTON
12 AUGUST 1999

ALAN WILDER
28 OCTOBER 1999

MARTHA LAVEY
01 SEPTEMBER 1999

FRANK GALATI
10 SEPTEMBER 1999

GARY COLE
28 OCTOBER 1999

RONDI REED
27 SEPTEMBER 1999

RANDALL ARNEY
04 AUGUST 1999

TINA LANDAU
21 FEBRUARY 2000

MOLLY REGAN
21 FEBRUARY 2000

RICK SNYDER
23 FEBRUARY 2000

ROBERT BREULER
03 MARCH 2000

MARIANN MAYBERRY
03 MARCH 2000

THE INDIAN WANTS THE BRONX 1976
PHOTOGRAPH: KEVIN RIGDON

ROSENCRANTZ AND GUILDENSTERN ARE DEAD 1977
PHOTOGRAPH: KEVIN RIGDON

HE CARETAKER 1978
HOTOGRAPH: LISA EBRIGHT

SAY GOODNIGHT, GRACIE 1979
PHOTOGRAPH: LISA EBRIGHT

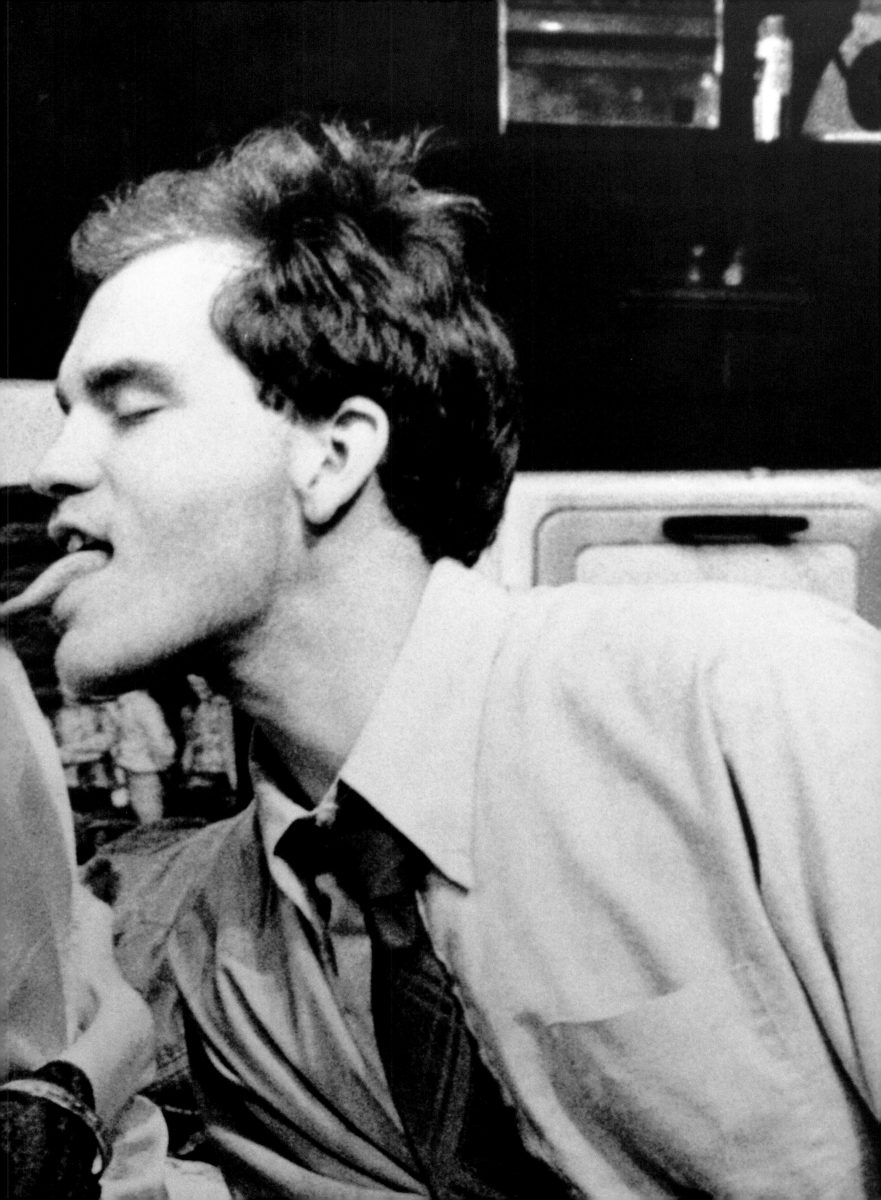

DON DeLILLO

Novelist Don DeLillo's LIBRA was adapted and directed by ensemble member John Malkovich during the 1993-1994 season. His second play, VALPARAISO, was produced in the 1999-2000 season under the direction of ensemble member Frank Galati.

"Finding The Dark Heart"

With dusty sunlight streaming in from the high windows, the two women in tights sat on the floor of the rehearsal hall, stretching and flexing, floating their arms in lazy arcs. They worked unselfconsciously, seemingly unaware of each other and of the three or four people just entering the hall after a break for a snack or smoke or a visit to the frontier toilet, equipped with hand-pump, that was situated behind a curtain, like a tiny experimental theater in Middle Europe.

A male member of the crew, struck by the other-worldliness of the two female actors in their dreamy gyrations, said to me, "They really are different from us, aren't they?"

Photograph: Michael Brosilow   **Libra 1994**

But I didn't think the difference was based on gender necessarily. Maybe it was just the great smoky space that separates actors in general from people in general, the rippling divide that makes theater so beautiful and elusive to a writer who has spent most of his time in the prison grip of the novel.

This was spring, 1994, and Steppenwolf was doing a stage version of my novel *Libra*, which John Malkovich had adapted and was now in the process of directing.

This is a story that deals at its heart with rootlessness and desperation. Through the passing days and nights of rehearsals and run-throughs, I began to get a sense of the company's own heart, whose chambers combine personal friendliness with a devotion to fearless theater, a willingness to extend the limits of stagecraft in order to address the far dark reaches of human behavior.

Six years later I would experience the Steppenwolf aura a second time with their production of *Valparaiso* under the expert and searching direction of Frank Galati.

Make the bet, take the risk, open the game to new levels. There's something very American about this and that's why Steppenwolf stands where it stands, at the spiritual heart of the country.

BALM IN GILEAD 1980
PHOTOGRAPH: LISA EBRIGHT

WAITING FOR THE PARADE 1981
PHOTOGRAPH: LISA EBRIGHT

TRACERS 1984
PHOTOGRAPH: LISA EBRIGHT

SAM SHEPARD

Steppenwolf Theatre Company has produced seven plays by Pulitzer Prize-winning playwright Sam Shepard. They include: ACTION (1981), TRUE WEST (1982), FOOL FOR LOVE (1984), COWBOY MOUTH (1984), A LIE OF THE MIND (1987), CURSE OF THE STARVING CLASS (1991) and BURIED CHILD (1995). Directed by ensemble member Gary Sinise, the Steppenwolf production of BURIED CHILD transferred from Chicago to New York in the spring of 1996 and featured ensemble members Terry Kinney, Lois Smith and Jim True.

"Guts"

Terry Kinney is throwing up in a bucket backstage at the Brooks Atkinson Theatre on Broadway. His whole body is shaking. It's dark back here and his skinny frame is silhouetted against the greenish light from the stage. I grab his arm and he looks into me with those deep, fullmoon eyes and tells me he tried what I suggested. I can't remember what it was I suggested and whatever it was I certainly didn't expect it to have had any disastrous effects on his health. "What was it?" I whisper.

"The ice." he says. "Remember? You told me that when Tilden goes out there it's like every step is on thin ice. He could go through any second."

"Oh, yeah," I say and he pukes again into the bucket; a silent puke so as not to disturb the actors on stage.

He's about to go on with an armload of carrots. The carrots are dripping mud all over his boots. Puke is dripping down his chin. He's shaking like it's forty below. I can't believe I'm somehow responsible for putting a human being through this.

"It's a scary world, Sam. Tilden lives in a scary world."

"Yeah, but I'm not sure it has to be this scary, Terry. I mean maybe it's not quite as scary as all this."

"Oh, it's this scary all right. It's at least this scary." And he heads for the open stage and thin ice.

Lois Smith is charging across the stage in a too-tight outfit; teetering in obviously painful high heels. Her whole character is bursting to get out of the confines of this costume, this set, this nightmare of family and heritage gone wild. It's an amazing thing to watch. There are times when a playwright is put to shame by an actor and this is one of them. When I watch Lois I can't help measuring the depth of the writing against the depth of the acting. It's there right in front of me. The desperation she brings to it is only hinted at on the page and yet she keeps pushing it, hunting for the tiniest crack where the dam might break. Her hair has come completely apart, Medusa fashion. Sweat pours down her back and arms. Her voice cracks into territories half way between the child and the woman; territories of total madness and yet the whole performance is somehow perfectly pitched and under control. I can't quite see how she's doing it. Usually I can manage to actually see what an actor is doing or at least understand the source where the character is emanating from but Lois is a mystery. She haunts the character. She stalks it. She comes into it from left field and leaves you gaping. There's layers going on. Layers and layers that keep sending

Buried Child 1995 *Photograph: Michael Brosilow*

waves of implication out to the audience and baffling the air around her. Through her performance I also begin to understand the extraordinary bravado of Gary's direction. He's encouraged this bald-faced daring in all the actors. Every one of them is pushing some limit and causing the play to take on an incarnation it's never had before. Suddenly connections are made, demons begin to emerge, a whole history of self-deception, fear and lying unfolds. It's as though the real inner core of the play has been discovered for the first time by simply pressing the material to its bursting point and then somehow containing the explosion inside a ravaged form that speaks directly to the emotions without frills, without excuses, beyond metaphor. After the performance my youngest daughter says to me about Lois: "Boy, that woman really has a lot of guts to wear that dress out there." "Guts" is the perfect term and may in fact come the closest to characterizing Steppenwolf, not just as a company of actors but as a whole mode of theater they have challenged us with.

LITTLE EGYPT 1987
PHOTOGRAPH: MICHAEL BROSILOW

THE GRAPES OF WRATH 1988
PHOTOGRAPH: MICHAEL BROSILOW

THE HOMECOMING 1989
PHOTOGRAPH: MICHAEL BROSILOW

RECKLESS 1990
PHOTOGRAPH: MICHAEL BROSILOW

KURT VONNEGUT

Kurt Vonnegut's novel SLAUGHTERHOUSE-5 was adapted and directed for Steppenwolf in 1996 by ensemble member Eric Simonson. In 1998, Mr. Vonnegut participated in Steppenwolf's TRAFFIC series in collaboration with Chicago's Orchestra X in the presentation of his new libretto for Stravinsky's "Histoire du Soldat." Later that year, Mr. Vonnegut returned for Steppenwolf's TRAFFIC presentation of Shostakovich's "Eighth Concerto," in which he recalled the bombing of Dresden.

"You Can Go Home Again"

There is a sort of immigrant in New York City who has no parades to celebrate the culture of his or her people and place of origin, who is not mentioned or even noticed by persons running for office, but who is nonetheless tremendously conceited about his or her homeland elsewhere, and critical of New York City. I speak of persons who have come from Chicago. Mike Nichols is a product of the University of Chicago, as am I, and I said to him last summer, "Chicago is a hell of a town," and he agreed most lustily. Nor would I have said that to him, and expected a warm reply, if it weren't for Lake Michigan, the University, the Chicago Art Institute, the Chicago Symphony Orchestra, the architecture of Louis Sullivan, and, since Mike's and my formative years, Steppenwolf.

Slaughterhouse-5 1996 Photograph: Michael Brosilow

Before I myself began to benefit personally from the existence of Steppenwolf, in what for me was emotionally a great big way, a welcome home, I liked all I heard and occasionally saw of Steppenwolf. It was so *organic,* as spiritually indigenous as a Prairie House by Frank Lloyd Wright. Steppenwolf was and is Chicago, and nowhere else. It was and is what theater used to be in ancient times, a part of the soul of a special community.

And then *wham!* Steppenwolf mounted the first dramatization of my novel *Slaughterhouse-5,* a production requiring such theatrical skills that it could not be published for use by amateur groups. And then *wham!* Steppenwolf, in collaboration with Chicago's organic, indigenous Orchestra X, made a success of my new libretto for Stravinsky's "Histoire du Soldat," which had received deservedly tepid reviews in New York City. And then *wham!* Again with Orchestra X, Steppenwolf provided a setting for a performance of Shostakovich's "Eighth Concerto," which the composer had dedicated to the victims of the Holocaust and the fire-bombing of Dresden, with my delivering prepared remarks about both calamities before and after, and during pauses in the tragical music.

Welcome home, indeed.

ANOTHER TIME 1991
PHOTOGRAPH: MICHAEL BROSILOW

THE SONG OF JACOB ZULU 1992
PHOTOGRAPH: MICHAEL BROSILOW

THE RISE AND FALL OF LITTLE VOICE 1993
PHOTOGRAPH: MICHAEL BROSILOW

A CLOCKWORK ORANGE 1994
PHOTOGRAPH: MICHAEL BROSILOW

AS I LAY DYING 1995
PHOTOGRAPH: MICHAEL BROSILOW

TERRY JOHNSON

In 1996, playwright and director Terry Johnson directed Stephen Jeffreys' play THE LIBERTINE on the Steppenwolf Mainstage featuring ensemble members John Malkovich, Alan Wilder, Francis Guinan, Mariann Mayberry and Martha Plimpton. During the 1999-2000 season, Steppenwolf produced Mr. Johnson's play HYSTERIA, under the direction of ensemble member John Malkovich.

"The Libertine, 1996"

In the 1920s, the blossoming English rail network designed a poster to advertise a small seaside town. It depicted a young boy in a howling gale, paddling on the edge of a choppy grey sea. It proclaimed that "Skegness is Bracing." Well, arriving in Chicago at two in the morning when they've lost your luggage and you're in your shirtsleeves is also pretty bracing. So is walking an ingenue's three-legged dog at midnight on the ice 'twixt lake and cityscape, but that's mere subplot.

Most bracing of all is stepping into a rehearsal room with Malkovich and the Steppenwolf ensemble. Remembering as one does so one's artistic director Martha Lavey's earlier impish whisper; "We're not going to have any... territorial disputes here are we?" I hadn't needed to search my soul. I reassured her and myself; a man as anxious and awed as I was is not about to make any pretence of being in charge.

Except, of course, I was. Steppenwolf, having decided that an English play in the Classical style should be directed by an English Classical director, had scoured the National Theatre and The Royal Shakespeare Company to no avail, but kept getting my name back on the "sorry, unavailable" faxes because I'd been chasing the game and begging favours. So now it was Stephen and I, The Royal Court meets the Chicago Ensemble. We're nervous, and swiftly overwhelmed. Not as we feared however, by adherence to a house style or years of familiarity or fame, but by the generosity of the welcome and the trust, and the genuine curiosity that is shown as to how we might intend to work on this play. Thus is uncovered the first secret of the Steppenwolf myth. The company is strong and thus generous. Wholly confident, therefore secure enough to let two unknown quantities into that confidence.

I discover *The Libertine* is the first period piece the company has performed in its twenty-five year history. We'd better do some sword practice. Malkovich has done a couple of swashbucklers, so we're soon waving rapiers around with frightening enthusiasm. Wearing them without falling over proves an altogether greater challenge. Rehearsal proper begins. Malkovich meanders. Speaks the text without much emphasis, as if throwing it away. He seems more interested in the props than in the meaning of the lines. It's deliberate of course; he's holding the sense as secondary to the minutiae of activity. He's circling the play. He's going to take it by surprise. Give Malkovich a rapier and a cup of coffee and the tip of the rapier will end up in the coffee. The coffee ends up in Al Wilder's face. (I was yet to discover this was as much tradition as inspiration). Give Malkovich his head and Mariann Mayberry and his head ends up between her thighs. The exploration reaches first base. I decide it's time to do some directing.

I suggest we replay a short scene, tidying up this move, polishing that. Malkovich pauses, then speaks at his quietest.

Malkovich: "Can I ask you something?" (Silence) "Are we *setting* this?"

Me: "Of course not." (I had been.) "I just thought we might, by way of experiment, try doing the same thing *twice*."

Malkovich: "Oh, well, that's fine. But if we're *setting* it, I think you should know that I *can't*."

Of course he can, but he doesn't have to, and he shouldn't. It's the Himalayas for Malkovich; the journey's meant to get harder, not easier, the nearer you get. I show the company some Hogarth prints and for a few days they Hogarth around, making vivid stage pictures that balance Malkovich's free-form Restoration style. Another signature of the ensemble; they're so relaxed and free with one another, the staging just happens. Instant RSC. If we were in Stratford-upon-Avon we could probably open now and get away with it.

I get over-confident. I ask them to improvise a croquet game on command. They stand in the wings. I give the command. Al Wilder shambles on, a croquet ball hits him on the head and he trips off in the other direction. The myth of the ensemble doesn't shatter, but I wonder if the glass is cracked. We laugh, however, and do it again, and it's not at all bad. I realise that if myth is nothing more

than an excellent gear shift, it's laughter and friendship that oils the machine.

I begin to realise what it is that Malkovich is looking for, and why I couldn't see it. He's looking for something *no one's ever seen before*. I begin to question my own artistic judgements. Do I "like" something, and try to set it because it's fresh and original or because I've seen it a hundred reassuring times before? Malkovich seduces us all into the search for the surprising, un-clichéd moment. It turns out he doesn't drink (except, apparently, on the first night of plays by Sam Shepard, and then only when he's in them). Our play's last scene depicts a man who's polished off two bottles of brandy. "How drunk's that?" he asks. He knows very well how drunk that is. The next time we get to the scene he walks on stone cold sober, the drunkest man I ever saw. He takes a few steps and falls flat on his face. His nose cracks the floor. He begins to say his lines. They are absolutely unintelligible. The attention gathers from the edges of the room. John is doing what Malkovich does. Missi Pyle, playing his wife, hits the deck soon after. She tries to make him sit up; she drops him. His head hits the floor again. He howls a despairing, raging torrent of alcohol-sodden desire and fury. He just discovered his character's in hell. She just discovered what acting is. He's on some plane where the deepest inner exploration has the most vivid outer expression. A young child paddling as a gale howls around him. He collapses. She wipes his face with her sleeve. The scene's finished.

It's traditional then for the director to say "Good" or even "Very good." This director can't think of a thing. "Coffee?" I suggest. Yes, smile the ensemble, as if coffee were the reason they came.

Postscript: Malkovich would later claim he was not in *mortal* agony, but very pissed at Missi, who was sitting on his foot.

THE LIBERTINE 1996
PHOTOGRAPH: MICHAEL BROSILOW

A STREETCAR NAMED DESIRE 1997
PHOTOGRAPH: MICHAEL BROSILOW

THE MEMORY OF WATER 199_
PHOTOGRAPH: MICHAEL BROSILOW

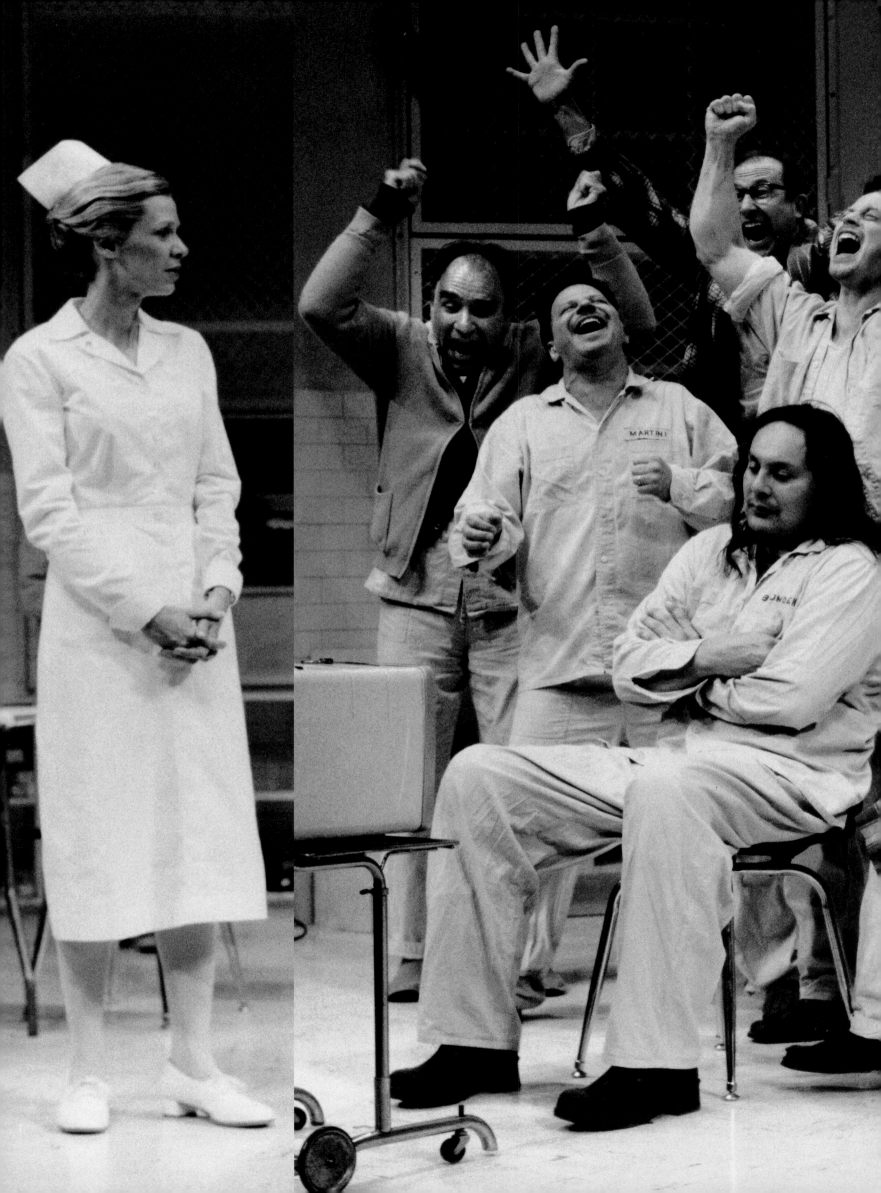

ONE FLEW OVER THE CUCKOO'S NEST 2000
PHOTOGRAPHS: MICHAEL BROSILOW

CHARLES L. MEE

Two plays by Charles L. Mee have been produced by Steppenwolf Theatre Company: TIME TO BURN in 1997 and the 1998 commissioned production of THE BERLIN CIRCLE. Both were directed by ensemble member Tina Landau.

"Risks"

When Martha Lavey said "we'd like to commission you to write something for next season," I started composing something in my head within a millisecond. Those words "for next season" have an astonishing, miraculous effect on a playwright. Most playwrights labor at a piece of writing for many months or years, mostly in despair that it will ever be any good or that anyone will ever want to put it on. The whole undertaking of writing plays normally feels hopeless and pointless, debilitating and exhausting, worthless and really stupid. And most theaters, when they do commission a play, do it without any plan to produce it, certainly without a schedule to produce it, and most often with an unspoken understanding that, in fact, they will never produce it—that they only want to commission it so that they can "develop" it and "workshop" it and then bury it so that they can say to themselves and to their patrons that they like to do new work.

But, to hear the words "for next season," to think someone is waiting for a script with the intention of putting it on (unless, it turns out, it is hopeless and pointless and worthless when it is finished) is immensely energizing. At once, I had a purpose, and a deadline, and an audience waiting to see what the play would be.

I took risks with the making of the piece I'd never otherwise have taken. I got up earlier in the mornings. I got to my desk right away. I felt a completely unjustified confidence and boldness and happiness in the work. And, not surprisingly, I think that confidence and happiness infused the play itself.

Martha asked if I would like to be given a workshop or any other sort of support in thinking about the piece—not that the play would be put into a workshop whether I wanted one or not, but rather, she asked me if I would like to develop some or all of the piece in the flesh. And when I said I would, she put together the money to afford a couple of weeks in a workshop conducted by my old friend and frequent collaborator, Tina Landau, who had directed three of my plays up to that time. Wonderful actors were brought into a room. And Tina, who writes plays herself and brings a terrifically happy and confident and positive frame of mind into a production, inspired the actors to invent things I'd never have thought of. Martha, and Steppenwolf's resident dramaturg Michele Volansky, and the resident director Anna Shapiro made lots of suggestions—never intrusively, always unassumingly, never thinking of how they would write a play but rather always how _this_ play wanted to be written. Never did someone want to display an ego, establish a pecking order, assume a superiority of knowledge or judgment:

The Berlin Circle 1998 Photograph: Michael Brosilow

always the work was served. Like Zen and the art of archery. The relationship of the workers to the work was unimpaired, clear.

And then, after I'd written another draft of the piece (or another hundred and seventeen drafts, as is my usual way of working), Martha brought everyone together again to read the play and look at it in its "final" form.

When a play of mine is produced, I hand the script to the director and leave town, and come back on opening night. I think a director and actors should be as free to do their thing as I was to do mine. And, if I am not there to pester people about being faithful to the script, they are unfettered to invent, to embellish, and to change what I've done. I feel if I've done my job right, the core of the piece will be clear—and whatever is not clear should be changed by those who see the shortcomings more lucidly than I do. And then, beyond that, the director and actors should be free to interpret and enrich and illuminate and re-create the piece as only they can. Of course, this is easy to say if you leave your script in the hands of Tina Landau. And Tina changed and sculpted and, with my blessing and gratitude, stayed up late, late at night rewriting passages of the piece right up to opening night. This is how _The Berlin Circle_ was written.

Lots of people talk about being supportive and nurturing, giving people the freedom to do their work, the emotional and financial support and the confidence to do it, extraordinary directors and actors and other collaborators to work with. In my experience, Steppenwolf is one of a tiny handful of theaters in the world that actually does this. This is how, and why, Steppenwolf produces new work.

K. TODD FREEMAN
22 MARCH 2000

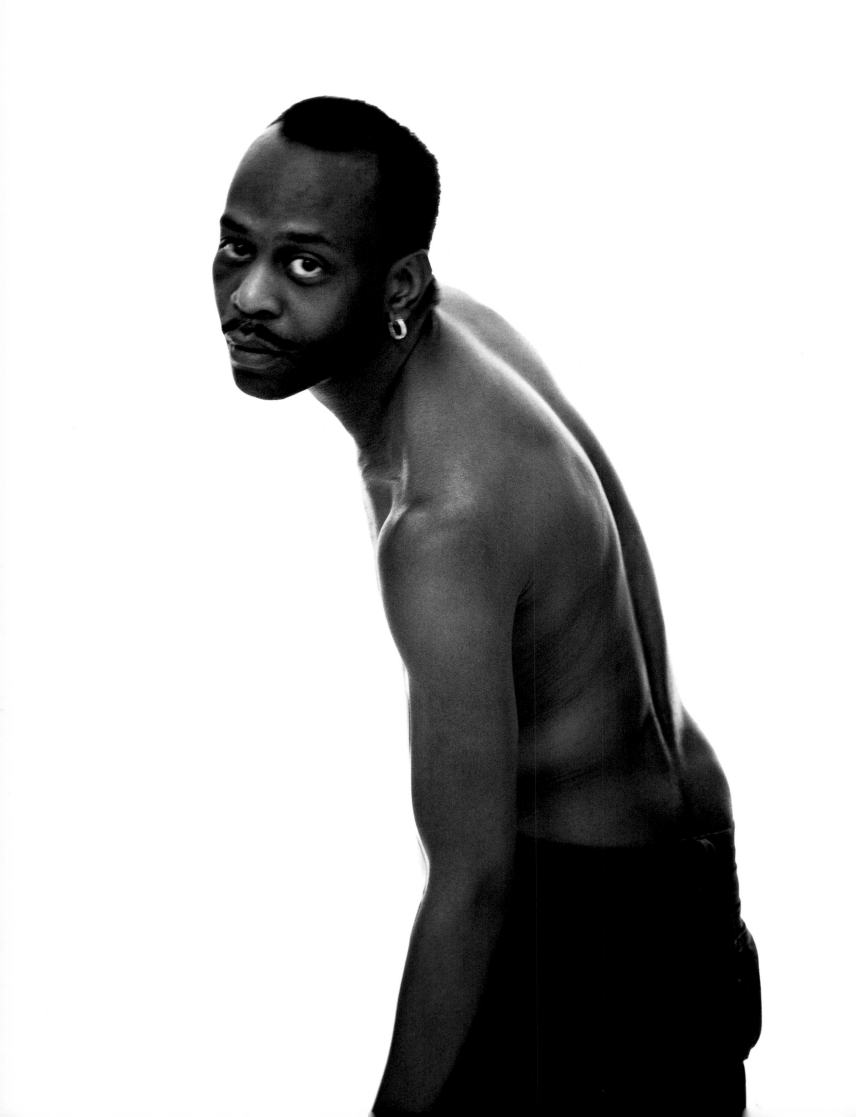

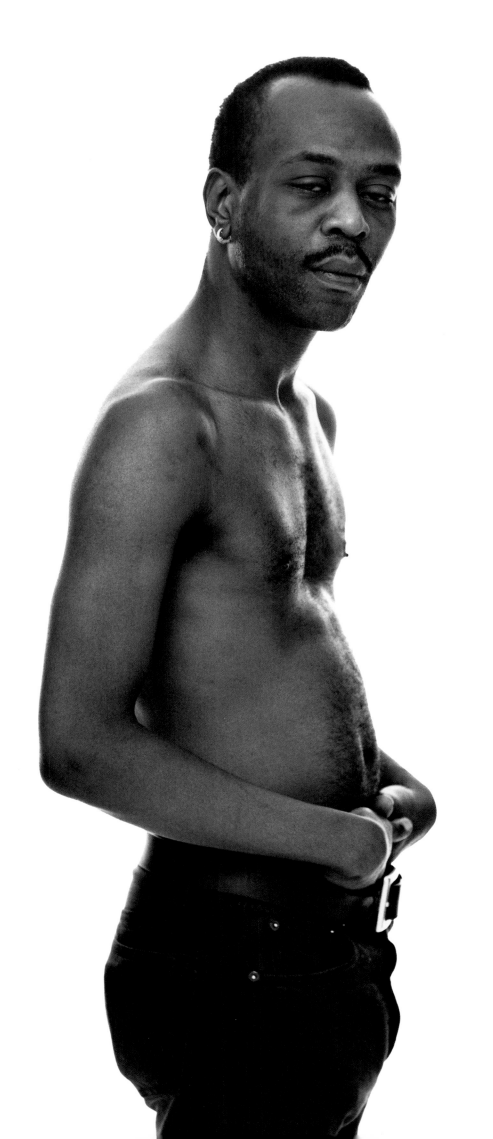

JIM TRUE-FROST
12 AUGUST 1999

KATHRYN ERBE
22 MARCH 2000

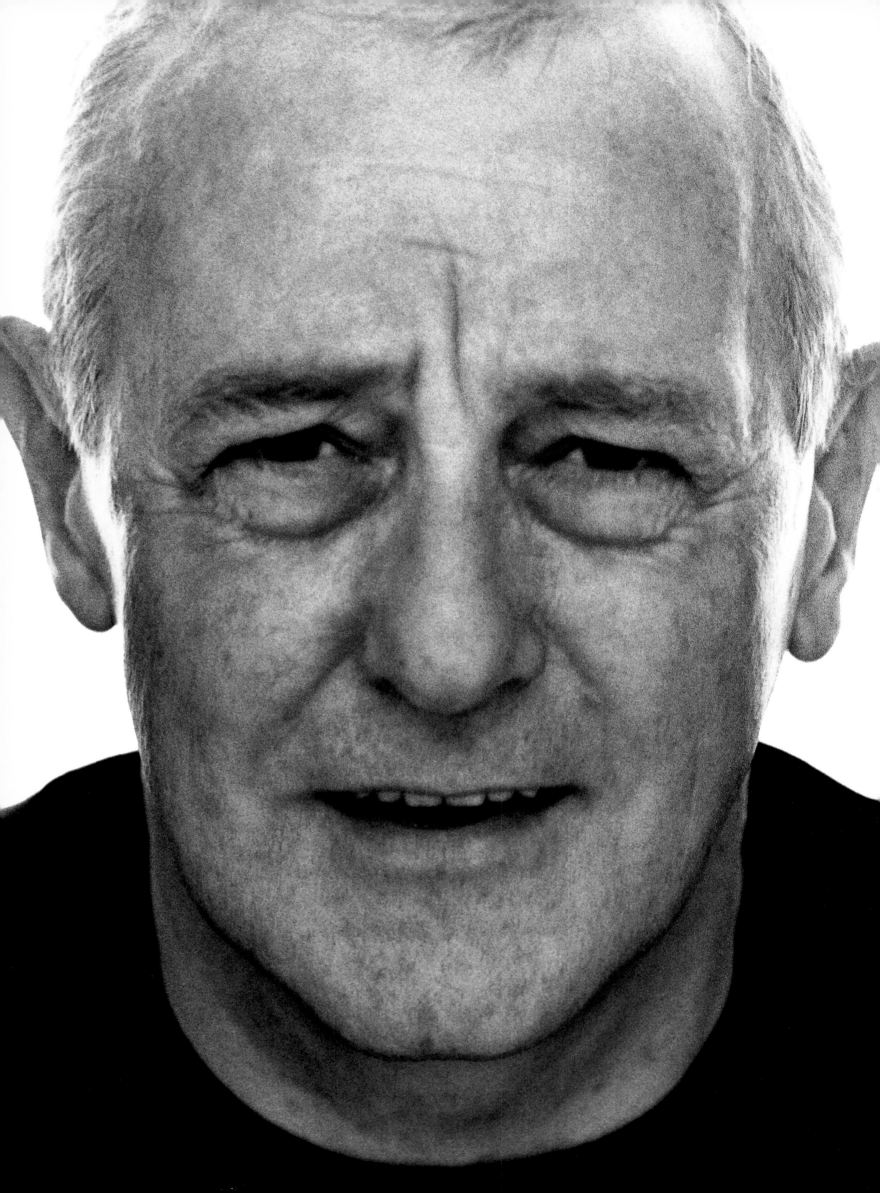

JOHN MAHONEY
10 APRIL 2000

GLENNE HEADLY
15 APRIL 2000

FRANCIS GUINAN
15 APRIL 2000

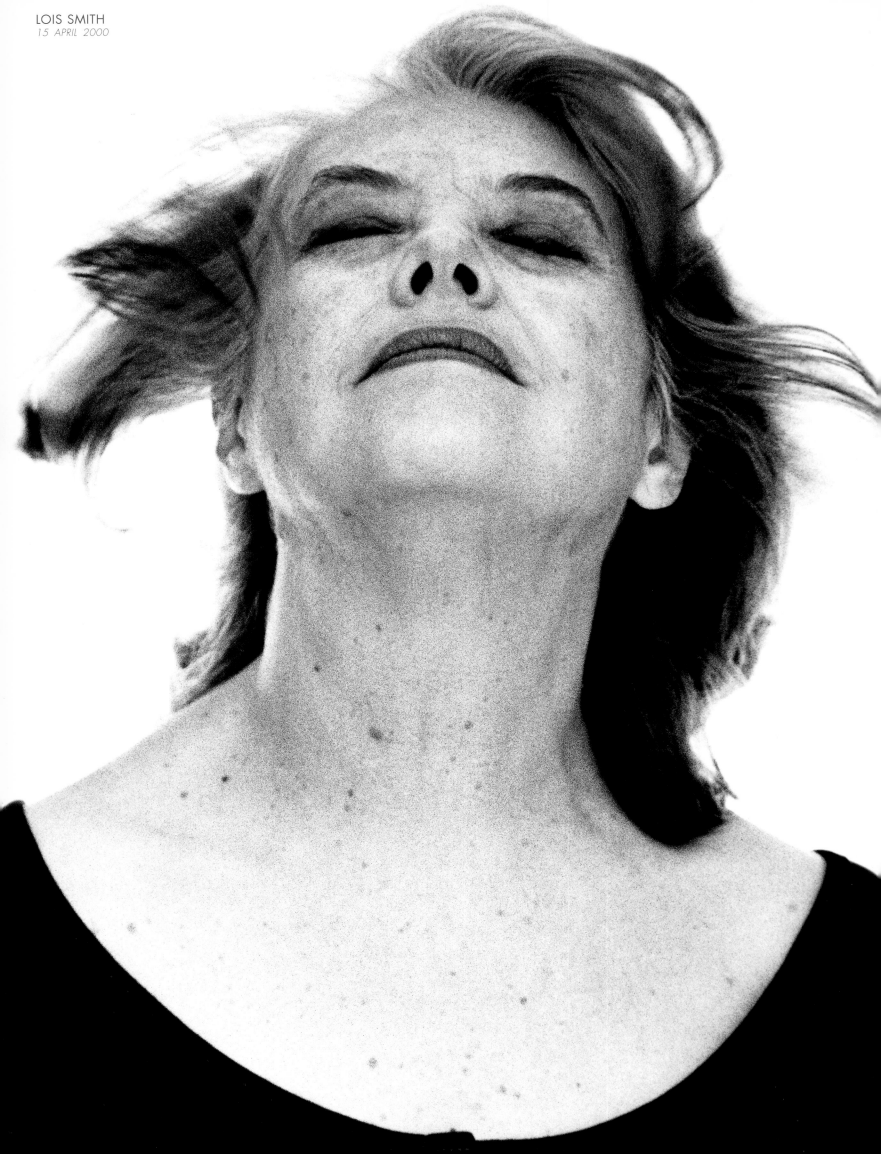

TOM IRWIN
17 APRIL 2000

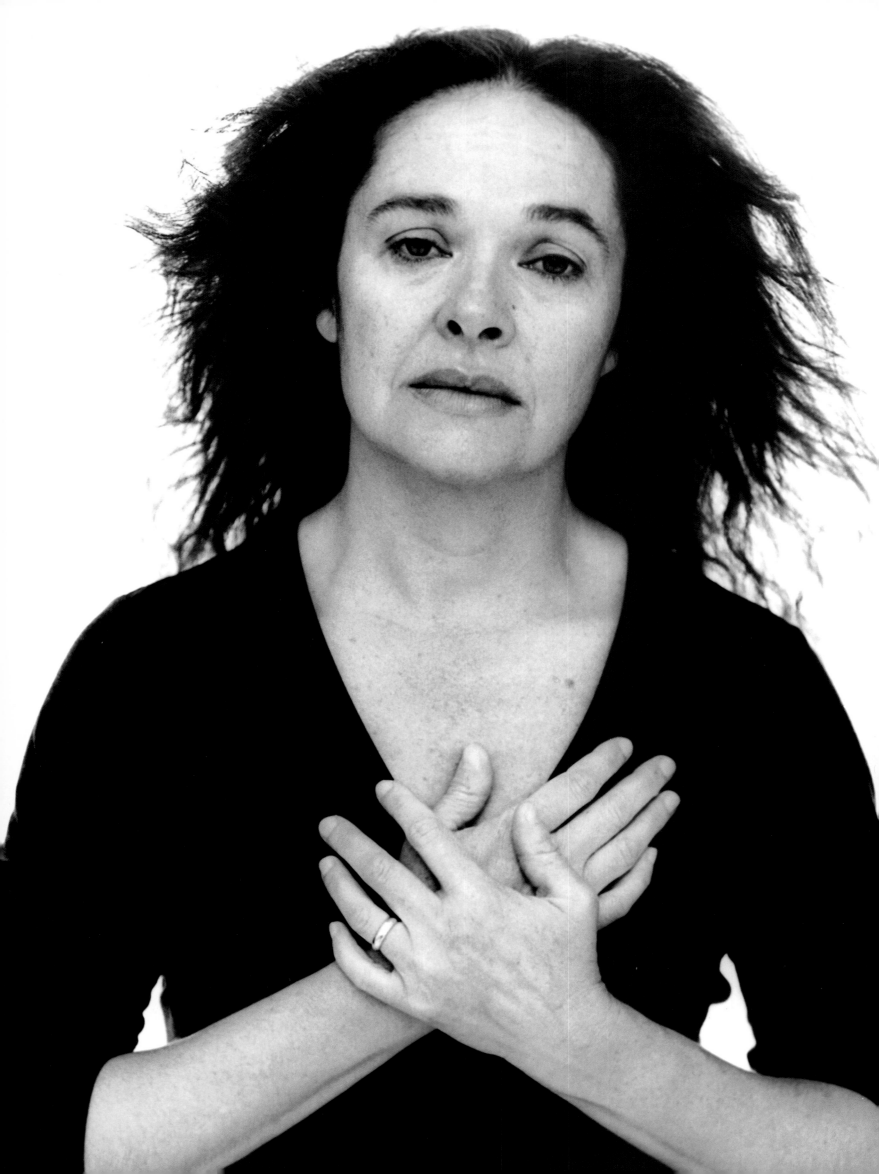

MOIRA HARRIS
17 APRIL 2000

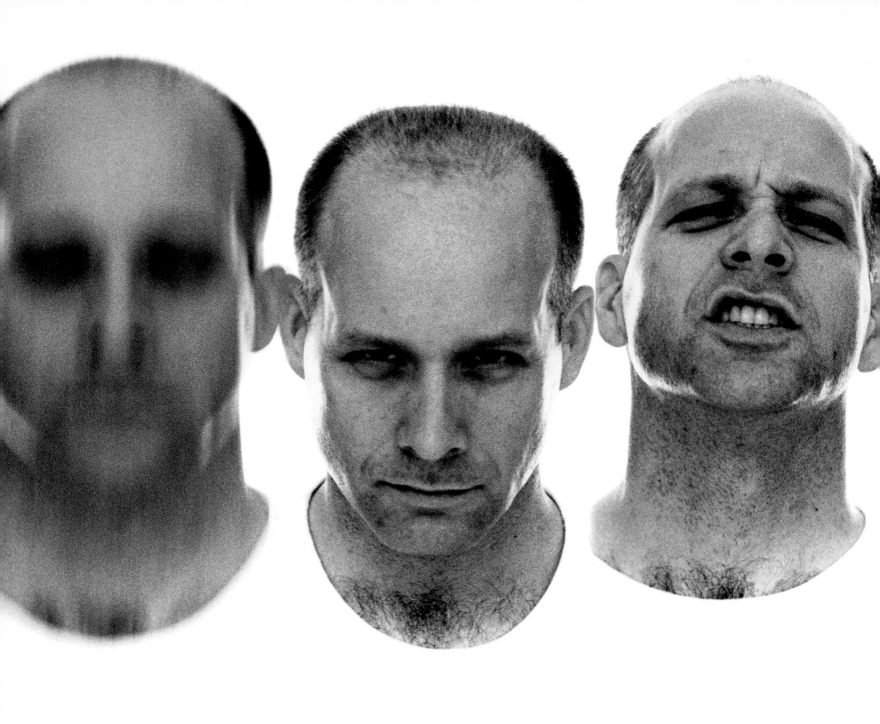

ERIC SIMONSON
15 APRIL 2000

PRODUCTION HISTORY

1974-2001

ARTISTIC DIRECTOR

Martha Lavey

EXECUTIVE DIRECTOR

Michael Gennaro

EXECUTIVE ARTISTIC BOARD

Terry Kinney

Jeff Perry

Gary Sinise

	PLAY	PLAYWRIGHT	DIRECTOR	LOCATION
1974				
Genesis of the company	And Miss Reardon Drinks a Little	Paul Zindel	Rick Argosh	North Shore Unitarian Church, Deerfield
	Grease	Jim Jacobs	Gary Sinise	Indian Trail School, Highland Park
	Rosencrantz and Guildenstern Are Dead	Tom Stoppard	Rick Argosh	North Shore Unitarian Church, Deerfield
	The Glass Menagerie	Tennessee Williams	Rick Argosh	Highland Park High School, Highland Park
1976-1977				
1st Season	The Lesson	Eugene Ionesco	Jeff Perry	1st Home: Steppenwolf Theatre Company 770 Deerfield Road, Highland Park
	The Indian Wants the Bronx	Israel Horovitz	John Malkovich	
	Birdbath	Leonard Melfi	H. E. Baccus	
	The Lover	Harold Pinter	Terry Kinney	
	Look, We've Come Through	Hugh Wheeler	H. E. Baccus	
	The Dumbwaiter	Harold Pinter	Nancy Evans & John Malkovich	
	The Loveliest Afternoon of the Year	John Guare	Jeff Perry	
	The Sea Horse	Edward J. Moore	John Malkovich	
	Birdbath (remount)	Leonard Melfi	H. E. Baccus	
	The Indian Wants the Bronx (remount)	Israel Horovitz	John Malkovich	
	Our Late Night	Wallace Shawn	Gary Houston	offsite: Jane Addams Hull House, Chicago
1977-1978				
2nd Season	Mack, Anything Goes Over the Rainbow*	adapted from the work of Harold Arlen, Cole Porter & Kurt Weill	H. E. Baccus	
	Rosencrantz and Guildenstern Are Dead	Tom Stoppard	Ralph Lane	
	Sandbar Flatland*	Daniel Ursini	John Malkovich	
	Home Free	Lanford Wilson	Terry Kinney	
	Krapp's Last Tape	Samuel Beckett	Jeff Perry	
	The Caretaker	Harold Pinter	John Malkovich	
1978-1979				
3rd Season	The 5th of July	Lanford Wilson	Steven Schachter	offsite: co-production at St. Nicholas Theater, Chicago
	Philadelphia, Here I Come!	Brian Friel	H. E. Baccus	
	Exit the King	Eugene Ionesco	Ralph Lane	offsite: Jane Addams Hull House, Chicago
	The Glass Menagerie	Tennessee Williams	H. E. Baccus	
	The Adventures of Mutt and Jeff* (childrens' show)	Rob Maxey	Rob Maxey	
1979-1980				
4th Season	Waiting for Lefty	Clifford Odets	Sheldon Patinkin	offsite: Apollo Theatre, Chicago
	Say Goodnight, Gracie	Ralph Pape	Austin Pendleton	offsite: Travel Light Theatre, Chicago
	Bonjour, La Bonjour	Michel Tremblay	H. E. Baccus	2nd Home: Steppenwolf Theatre Company 3212 N. Broadway, Chicago
	Death of a Salesman	Arthur Miller	Sheldon Patinkin	
	Quiet Jeannie Green*	Daniel Ursini	H. E. Baccus	
	The Collection (late night series)	Harold Pinter	Stephen B. Eich	
	The Dock Brief (late night series)	John Mortimer	Jane Perry	
1980-1981				
5th Season	Balm in Gilead	Lanford Wilson	John Malkovich	
	Absent Friends	Alan Ayckbourn	H. E. Baccus & John Malkovich	
	Savages	Christopher Hampton	John Malkovich	
	Arms and the Man	George Bernard Shaw	Sheldon Patinkin	
	No Man's Land	Harold Pinter	John Malkovich	
	Balm in Gilead (remount)	Lanford Wilson	John Malkovich	offsite: Apollo Theatre, Chicago
	Action (late night series)	Sam Shepard	Gary Sinise	
	The Great American Desert (late night series)	Joel Oppenheimer	Stephen B. Eich	
	The Littlest Elf* (childrens' show)	Rob Maxey (book) Robert Biggs (music/lyrics)	Rob Maxey	offsite: First Chicago Center, Chicago
	Morning Call (live TV)	Alan Gross	Gary Sinise	offsite: Travel Light Theatre, Chicago
1981-1982				
6th Season	Of Mice and Men	John Steinbeck	Terry Kinney	
	Waiting for the Parade	John Murrell	Gary Sinise	
	Loose Ends	Michael Weller	Austin Pendleton	
	True West	Sam Shepard	Gary Sinise	
	The House	David Halliwell	John Malkovich	
	True West (remount)	Sam Shepard	Gary Sinise	offsite: Apollo Theatre, Chicago
	Big Mother (late night series)	Charles Dizenzo	Laurie Metcalf	
	The Coarse Acting Show (late night series)	Michael Green	John Mahoney	offsite: Cross Currents Theatre, Chicago
1982-1983				
7th Season	A Prayer for My Daughter	Thomas Babe	John Malkovich	3rd Home: Steppenwolf Theatre Company 2851 N. Halsted, Chicago
	And a Nightingale Sang...	C. P. Taylor	Terry Kinney	
	Cloud 9	Caryl Churchill	Don Amendolia	
	A Moon for the Misbegotten	Eugene O'Neill	Jeff Perry	
	The Miss Firecracker Contest	Beth Henley	Gary Sinise	

*world premiere production

	PLAY	PLAYWRIGHT	DIRECTOR	LOCATION
1983-1984				
8th Season	The Hothouse	Harold Pinter	Jeff Perry	
	Our Town	Thornton Wilder	Ralph Lane	
	Tracers	John DiFusco	Gary Sinise	
	Fool for Love	Sam Shepard	Terry Kinney	
	Cowboy Mouth (late night series)	Sam Shepard	Phyllis Schuringa	
	Canadian Gothic (late night series)	Joanna Glass	Glenne Headly	
	'dentity Crisis (late night series)	Christopher Durang	Cary Libkin	
1984-1985				
9th Season	Stage Struck	Simon Gray	Tom Irwin	
	The Three Sisters	Anton Chekhov (translated by Lanford Wilson)	Austin Pendleton	
	Orphans	Lyle Kessler	Gary Sinise	
	Coyote Ugly*	Lynn Siefert	John Malkovich	
	Miss Julie	August Strindberg	Tom Irwin	
	La Ronde (late night series)	Arthur Schnitzler	Keith Miller	
1985-1986				
10th Season	The Caretaker	Harold Pinter	John Malkovich	
	You Can't Take It With You	Moss Hart & George S. Kaufman	Frank Galati	
	A Lesson from Aloes	Athol Fugard	Suzanne Shepard	
	Lydie Breeze	John Guare	Rondi Reed	
	Frank's Wild Years*	Tom Waits & Kathleen Brennan	Gary Sinise	offsite: Briar Street Theatre, Chicago
1986-1987				
11th Season	Bang	Laura Cunningham	Randall Arney	
	Cat on a Hot Tin Roof	Tennessee Williams	Austin Pendleton	
	Educating Rita	Willy Russell	Jeff Perry	
	A Lie of the Mind	Sam Shepard	Julie Hébert	
	Aunt Dan and Lemon	Wallace Shawn	Frank Galati	
1987-1988				
12th Season	Burn This	Lanford Wilson	Marshall W. Mason	offsite: Royal George Theatre, Chicago
	Little Egypt*	Lynn Siefert	Jeff Perry	
	Born Yesterday	Garson Kanin	Frank Galati	
	The Common Pursuit	Simon Gray	Rondi Reed	
	Killers	John Olive	Randall Arney	
1988-1989				
13th Season	The Grapes of Wrath*	Frank Galati (adapted from John Steinbeck)	Frank Galati	offsite: Royal George Theatre, Chicago
	Stepping Out	Richard Harris	Rondi Reed	offsite: Ivanhoe Theatre, Chicago
	A Walk in the Woods	Lee Blessing	Randall Arney	
	Ring Round the Moon	Jean Anouilh (translated by Christopher Fry)	Rondi Reed	
	El Salvador	Rafael Lima	Francis Guinan	
	Terry Won't Talk (late night series)	Mark Leib	Jim True	
1989-1990				
14th Season	The Homecoming	Harold Pinter	Jeff Perry	
	The Geography of Luck*	Marlane Meyer	Randall Arney	
	Reckless	Craig Lucas	Terry Kinney	
	Love Letters	A. R. Gurney	Randall Arney & Stephen B. Eich	
	Wrong Turn at Lungfish*	Garry Marshall & Lowell Ganz	Garry Marshall	offsite: Apollo Theatre, Chicago
1990-1991				
15th Season	The Secret Rapture	David Hare	Eric Simonson	offsite: Apollo Theatre, Chicago
	Harvey	Mary Chase	Austin Pendleton	offsite: Apollo Theatre, Chicago
	Another Time	Ronald Harwood	Ronald Harwood	4th Home: Steppenwolf Theatre Company 1650 N. Halsted, Chicago, Mainstage
	Curse of the Starving Class	Sam Shepard	Randall Arney	Mainstage
	Earthly Possessions*	Frank Galati (adapted from Anne Tyler)	Frank Galati	Mainstage
	Tennessee (late night series)	Romulus Linney	Jim True	offsite: 2851 N. Halsted, Chicago
	Bite the Hand (late night series)	Ara Watson	Jim True	offsite: 2851 N. Halsted, Chicago
1991-1992				
16th Season	Your Home in the West	Rod Wooden	Tom Irwin	Mainstage
	A Summer Remembered	Charles Nolte	Stephen B. Eich	Mainstage
	A Slip of the Tongue*	Dusty Hughes	Simon Stokes	Mainstage
	The Song of Jacob Zulu*	Tug Yourgrau	Eric Simonson	Mainstage
	My Thing of Love*	Alexandra Gersten	Terry Kinney	Mainstage
1992-1993				
17th Season	Awake and Sing!	Clifford Odets	Sheldon Patinkin	Mainstage
	Inspecting Carol	Daniel Sullivan	Eric Simonson	Mainstage
	The Song of Jacob Zulu (remount)	Tug Yourgrau	Eric Simonson	Mainstage
	The Road to Nirvana	Arthur Kopit	Gary Sinise	Mainstage
	Ghost in the Machine*	David Gilman	Jim True	Mainstage
	Death and the Maiden	Ariel Dorfman	Randall Arney	Mainstage

*world premiere production

	PLAY	PLAYWRIGHT	DIRECTOR	LOCATION
1993-1994				
18th Season	Evelyn and the Polka King	John Olive	Eric Simonson	Mainstage
	The Rise and Fall of Little Voice	Jim Cartwright	Simon Curtis	Mainstage
	The Mesmerist	Ara Watson	Jim True	Mainstage
	Libra*	John Malkovich (adapted from Don DeLillo)	John Malkovich	Mainstage
	Talking Heads	Alan Bennett	John Mahoney	Mainstage
	Picasso at the Lapin Agile*	Steve Martin	Randall Arney	Studio
1994-1995				
19th Season	A Clockwork Orange*	Anthony Burgess	Terry Kinney	Mainstage
	Playland	Athol Fugard	Jonathan Wilson	Mainstage
	Time of My Life	Alan Ayckbourn	Michael Maggio	Mainstage
	Nomathemba (Hope)*	Ntozake Shange, Joseph Shabalala, Eric Simonson	Eric Simonson	Mainstage
	As I Lay Dying*	Frank Galati (adapted from William Faulkner)	Frank Galati	Mainstage
	Slavs!	Tony Kushner	Eric Simonson	Studio
	Uncle Bob*	Austin Pendleton	Kelly Morgan	Studio
1995-1996				
20th Season	Buried Child	Sam Shepard	Gary Sinise	Mainstage
	Everyman	Anonymous (edited by A.C. Cawley)	Frank Galati	Mainstage
	The Libertine	Stephen Jeffreys	Terry Johnson	Mainstage
	Supple in Combat*	Alexandra Gersten-Vassilaros	Max Mayer	Mainstage
	Molly Sweeney	Brian Friel	Kyle Donnelly	Mainstage
	The Cryptogram	David Mamet	Scott Zigler	Studio
1996-1997				
21st Season	Slaughterhouse-5*	Eric Simonson (adapted from Kurt Vonnegut)	Eric Simonson	Mainstage
	Mojo	Jez Butterworth	Ian Rickson	Mainstage
	Time to Burn*	Charles L. Mee	Tina Landau	Mainstage
	A Streetcar Named Desire	Tennessee Williams	Terry Kinney	Mainstage
	A Fair Country	Jon Robin Baitz	Scott Zigler	Mainstage
	The Viewing Room*	Daniel J. Rubin	Anna D. Shapiro	Studio
	The Designated Mourner	Wallace Shawn	Les Waters	Studio
1997-1998				
22nd Season	Skylight	David Hare	Mike Nussbaum	Mainstage
	Space*	Tina Landau	Tina Landau	Mainstage
	The Memory of Water	Shelagh Stephenson	Les Waters	Mainstage
	The Man Who Came to Dinner	Moss Hart & George S. Kaufman	James Burrows	Mainstage
	The Playboy of the Western World	J. M. Synge	Douglas Hughes	Mainstage (co-production with Long Wharf Theatre)
	Goodbye Stranger*	Carrie Luft	Polly Noonan	Studio
	Pot Mom	Justin Tanner	Wilson Milam	Studio
	Wolf Lullaby	Hilary Bell	Anna D. Shapiro	Garage
1998-1999				
23rd Season	The Berlin Circle*	Charles L. Mee	Tina Landau	Mainstage
	The Glass Menagerie	Tennessee Williams	Mark Brokaw	Mainstage
	Three Days of Rain	Richard Greenberg	Anna D. Shapiro	Mainstage
	Morning Star	Sylvia Regan	Frank Galati	Mainstage
	The Beauty Queen of Leenane	Martin McDonagh	Randall Arney	Mainstage
	Mizlansky/Zilinsky or Schmucks	Jon Robin Baitz	Amy Morton	Studio
	Tavern Story*	David VanMatre	Rick Snyder	Garage
1999-2000				
24th Season	Side Man	Warren Leight	Anna D. Shapiro	Mainstage
	Hysteria	Terry Johnson	John Malkovich	Mainstage
	Valparaiso	Don DeLillo	Frank Galati	Mainstage
	One Flew Over the Cuckoo's Nest	Dale Wasserman (adapted from Ken Kesey)	Terry Kinney	Mainstage
	Closer	Patrick Marber	Abigail Deser	Mainstage
	The Infidel*	Bruce Norris	Anna D. Shapiro	Studio
	Orson's Shadow*	Austin Pendleton	David Cromer	Garage
	Detail of a Larger Work*	Lisa Dillman	Robin Stanton	Garage
2000-2001				
25th Season	The Ballad of Little Jo*	Sarah Schlesinger (words) Mike Reid (music)	Tina Landau	Mainstage
	The Weir	Conor McPherson	Amy Morton	Mainstage
	David Copperfield*	Giles Havergal (adapted from Charles Dickens)	Giles Havergal	Mainstage
	The Drawer Boy	Michael Healey	Anna D. Shapiro	Mainstage
	Hedda Gabler	Henrik Ibsen	Douglas Hughes	Mainstage (co-production with Long Wharf Theatre)
	Uncle Vanya	Anton Chekhov (translated by Curt Columbus)	Sheldon Patinkin	Studio
	The Ordinary Yearnings of Miriam Buddwing*	Alexandra Gersten-Vassilaros	Anna D. Shapiro	Studio
	The House of Lily*	Lydia Stryk	Curt Columbus	Garage

*world premiere production

PRODUCTIONS TRANSFERRED TO OTHER THEATERS

1982	*True West*	Cherry Lane Theatre, New York
1983	*And a Nightingale Sang . . .*	Lincoln Center, New York
1984	*Balm in Gilead*	Circle Repertory Theatre, New York
1984	*Balm in Gilead*	Minetta Lane Theatre, New York
1985	*And a Nightingale Sang . . .*	Alliance Theatre, Atlanta
1985	*Orphans*	Westside Arts Theater, New York
1985	*Coyote Ugly*	Kennedy Center, Washington D.C.
1985	*Streamers*	Kennedy Center, Washington D.C.
1986	*Orphans*	Hampstead Theatre, London
1986	*Orphans*	Apollo Theatre, London
1986	*The Caretaker*	Circle in the Square Theatre, New York
1987	*Lydie Breeze*	Festivals of Sydney and Perth, Australia
1987	*Educating Rita*	Westside Arts Theater, New York
1989	*The Grapes of Wrath*	La Jolla Playhouse, California
1989	*The Grapes of Wrath*	Royal National Theatre, London
1990	*The Grapes of Wrath*	Cort Theatre, New York
1992	*A Slip of the Tongue*	Shaftesbury Theatre, London
1993	*The Song of Jacob Zulu*	Festival of Perth, Australia
1993	*The Song of Jacob Zulu*	Plymouth Theatre, New York
1994	*The Rise and Fall of Little Voice*	Neil Simon Theatre, New York
1994	*Picasso at the Lapin Agile*	Westwood Playhouse, Los Angeles
1996	*Buried Child*	Brooks Atkinson Theatre, New York
1996	*Nomathemba (Hope)*	Kennedy Center, Washington D.C
1998	*The Man Who Came to Dinner*	Barbican Centre, London
1998	*The Playboy of the Western World*	Long Wharf Theatre, Connecticut
1999	*Space*	Mark Taper Forum, Los Angeles
1999	*Space*	Joseph Papp Public Theatre, New York
2000	*The Berlin Circle*	American Repertory Theatre, Massachusetts
2000	*Orson's Shadow*	Williamstown Theatre Festival, Massachusetts
2000	*Orson's Shadow*	Westport Playhouse, Connecticut
2000	*Side Man*	Galway Arts Festival, Ireland
2000	*One Flew Over the Cuckoo's Nest*	Barbican Centre, London

AWARDS
National/Regional

1983	Obie Award for Off-Broadway Excellence as a Director: Gary Sinise for *True West*
1983	Obie Award for Off-Broadway Excellence as an Actor: John Malkovich for *True West*
1983	Clarence Derwent Award for Most Promising Actor: John Malkovich for *True West*
1984	Clarence Derwent Award for Most Promising Actress: Joan Allen for *And a Nightingale Sang . . .*
1985	Tony Award for Regional Theatre Excellence
1985	Drama Desk Award for Outstanding Director: John Malkovich for *Balm in Gilead*
1985	Theatre World Award for Outstanding New Talent Off-Broadway: Laurie Metcalf for *Balm in Gilead*
1985	Theatre World Award for Outstanding New Talent Off-Broadway: Kevin Anderson for *Orphans*
1985	Theatre World Award for Outstanding New Talent Off-Broadway: John Mahoney for *Orphans*
1985	Obie Award for Off-Broadway Excellence as a Director: John Malkovich for *Balm in Gilead*
1985	Obie Award for Off-Broadway Excellence as an Actress: Laurie Metcalf for *Balm in Gilead*
1986	Clarence Derwent Award for Most Promising Actor: John Mahoney for *Orphans*
1988	Tony Award for Best Actress: Joan Allen for *Burn This*
1990	Tony Award for Best Play: *The Grapes of Wrath*
1990	Tony Award for Best Director: Frank Galati for *The Grapes of Wrath*
1990	Drama Desk Award for Best Play: *The Grapes of Wrath*
1990	Drama Desk Award for Best Director: Frank Galati for *The Grapes of Wrath*
1990	Outer Critics Circle Award for Outstanding Broadway Play: *The Grapes of Wrath*
1998	National Medal of Arts
2000	Illinois Arts Legend Award
2000	Gradiva Award from the National Association for the Advancement of Psychoanalysis: John Malkovich for *Hysteria*

Joseph Jefferson Awards for Chicago Theater Excellence

1979	*The Glass Menagerie*: Laurie Metcalf, Supporting Actress
1980	*Say Goodnight, Gracie*: Ensemble
1980	*Say Goodnight, Gracie*: Glenne Headly, Supporting Actress
1981	*Balm in Gilead*: Production
1981	*Balm in Gilead*: Ensemble
1981	*Balm in Gilead*: John Malkovich, Director
1981	*Balm in Gilead*: Laurie Metcalf, Actress
1981	*Balm in Gilead*: Glenne Headly, Supporting Actress
1981	*Balm in Gilead*: Debra Engle, Cameo Appearance
1981	*Balm in Gilead*: Kevin Rigdon, Lighting Design
1982	*True West*: John Malkovich, Actor
1982	*The House*: Ensemble
1982	*Waiting for the Parade*: Rondi Reed, Supporting Actress
1983	*And a Nightingale Sang . . .*: Terry Kinney, Director
1983	*And a Nightingale Sang . . .*: Joan Allen, Actress
1983	*Cloud 9*: Ensemble
1983	*The Miss Firecracker Contest*: Glenne Headly, Supporting Actress
1984	*Tracers*: Ensemble
1984	*Tracers*: Christian Peterson, Sound Effects Design
1985	*Orphans*: Production
1985	*Orphans*: Ensemble
1985	*Orphans*: Gary Sinise, Director
1985	*Orphans*: Kevin Anderson, Actor
1985	*Coyote Ugly*: Laurie Metcalf, Actress
1985	*Coyote Ugly*: Glenne Headly, Supporting Actress
1986	*A Lesson from Aloes*: Joan Allen, Actress
1986	*You Can't Take it With You*: Ensemble
1986	*You Can't Take it With You*: Frank Galati, Director
1986	*You Can't Take it With You*: Laurie Metcalf, Cameo Performance
1987	*Bang*: Gary Cole, Actor
1987	*Educating Rita*: Laurie Metcalf, Actress
1988	*The Common Pursuit*: Ensemble
1988	*Killers*: Jim True, Supporting Actor
1989	*A Walk in the Woods*: Robert Breuler, Actor
1989	*The Grapes of Wrath*: Production
1989	*The Grapes of Wrath*: Frank Galati, New Work
1989	*The Grapes of Wrath*: Frank Galati, Director
1989	*The Grapes of Wrath*: Rob Milburn, Sound Design
1989	*Stepping Out*: Ensemble
1991	*Another Time*: Albert Finney, Actor
1991	*Another Time*: Molly Regan, Supporting Actress
1992	*My Thing of Love*: Laurie Metcalf, Actress
1992	*My Thing of Love*: Alexandra Gersten, New Work
1992	*The Song of Jacob Zulu*: Tug Yourgrau, New Work
1994	*Libra*: Laurie Metcalf, Supporting Actress
1995	*A Clockwork Orange*: Kevin Rigdon, Lighting Design
1995	*A Clockwork Orange*: Robert Brill, Scenic Design
1995	*A Clockwork Orange*: Rob Milburn and Michael Bodeen, Sound Design
1995	*Nomathemba (Hope)*: Joseph Shabalala, Original Music
1996	*Buried Child*: Gary Sinise, Director
1996	*Buried Child*: James Gammon, Principal Actor
1996	*Buried Child*: Robert Brill, Scenic Design
1996	*Supple in Combat*: Linda Stephens, Actress in Cameo
1997	*A Streetcar Named Desire*: Laila Robins, Principal Actress
1997	*A Streetcar Named Desire*: Kevin Rigdon, Lighting Design
1997	*Time to Burn*: Ensemble
1997	*Time to Burn*: Scott Zielinski, Lighting Design
1998	*Space*: Scott Zielinski, Lighting Design
1999	*Morning Star*: Yasen Peyankov, Supporting Actor

AMY MORTON

Ensemble member since 1997. Steppenwolf: Actress: *One Flew Over the Cuckoo's Nest* (also London); *Three Days of Rain; The Berlin Circle; The Memory of Water; Space* (also Off-Broadway); *A Streetcar Named Desire; The Cryptogram; Slavs!; Love Letters; The Geography of Luck; A Lie of the Mind; You Can't Take it With You.* Director: *Mizlansky/Zilinsky or Schmucks.* Other Stage including: Member of Remains Theatre Company for 15 years; Actress: Guthrie Theatre: *Pravda;* Goodman Theatre: *A Flea in Her Ear; Unjustifiable Acts; Sin; The Time of Your Life;* Wisdom Bridge Theatre: *Life and Limb;* Victory Gardens Theatre: *Flyovers.* Director: Remains Theatre: *Our Country's Good.* Film: *8MM; Rookie of the Year; Backdraft; Falling Down.* Birthplace: Oak Park, Illinois.

ALAN WILDER

Ensemble member since 1976. Steppenwolf: *Side Man* (also Ireland); *The Man Who Came to Dinner* (also London); *The Libertine; Everyman; Talking Heads; The Rise and Fall of Little Voice; Inspecting Carol; Awake and Sing!; The Song of Jacob Zulu* (also Broadway, Australia); *Earthly Possessions; Curse of the Starving Class; Love Letters; Reckless; The Geography of Luck; The Homecoming; The Grapes of Wrath* (also Broadway, London, La Jolla); *The Common Pursuit; Born Yesterday; Aunt Dan and Lemon; Cat on a Hot Tin Roof; Frank's Wild Years; You Can't Take it With You; The Caretaker* (also Broadway); *Streamers* (Kennedy Center); *The Three Sisters; Stage Struck; Tracers; Our Town; The Hothouse; A Moon for the Misbegotten; Cloud 9; And a Nightingale Sang...; The House; Loose Ends; Arms and the Man; Savages; Absent Friends; Balm in Gilead; Death of a Salesman; Waiting for Lefty; The Caretaker; Exit the King; Philadelphia, Here I Come!; Krapp's Last Tape; Rosencrantz and Guildenstern Are Dead; Mack, Anything Goes Over the Rainbow; Our Late Night; The Lesson.* Other Stage including: Westwood Playhouse: *Picasso at the Lapin Agile;* Guthrie Theatre: *Pravda;* Remains Theatre: *Highest Standard of Living;* Lyric Opera of Chicago: *The Merry Widow;* Wisdom Bridge Theatre: *The Importance of Being Earnest; Travesties.* Film: *A Civil Action; Deep Impact; Kiss the Girls; A League of Their Own; Sour Grapes; Home Alone; Child's Play; Betrayed.* Television: *L.A. Sheriff's Homicide; Always Outnumbered; The Practice; George and Leo; Frasier; Murphy Brown; Public Morals; Cybill; Party of Five; Dave's World; Mad About You.* Birthplace: Chicago, Illinois.

B I O G R A P H I E S

Ensemble member since 1976. Steppenwolf: *The Beauty Queen of Leenane; Pot Mom; Libra; My Thing of Love* (also Broadway); *Wrong Turn at Lungfish; Love Letters; Killers; Little Egypt; Educating Rita* (also Off-Broadway); *You Can't Take it With You; Coyote Ugly* (also Kennedy Center); *The Miss Firecracker Contest; Cloud 9; And a Nightingale Sang...; True West; Loose Ends; Waiting for the Parade; Arms and the Man; Savages; Absent Friends; Balm in Gilead* (also Off-Broadway); *Quiet Jeanie Green; Bonjour, La Bonjour; Waiting for Lefty; The Glass Menagerie; Exit the King; The 5th of July; Home Free; Sandbar Flatland; Rosencrantz and Guildenstern Are Dead; Mack, Anything Goes Over the Rainbow; The Sea Horse; The Lover.* Other Stage including: Off-Broadway: *Bodies, Rest and Motion;* Williamstown Theatre Festival: *School for Scandal;* Wisdom Bridge Theatre: *Getting Out;* Northlight Theatre: *Who's Afraid of Virginia Woolf?;* Columbia College, Chicago: *The Man Who Came to Dinner; Member of the Wedding.* Film: *Runaway Bride; Toy Story; Scream II; Bulworth; Blink; Leaving Las Vegas; Chicago Cab; U-Turn; Dear God; A Dangerous Woman; JFK; Mistress; Pacific Heights; Internal Affairs; Uncle Buck; Miles From Home; Stars and Bars; Making Mr. Right; Desperately Seeking Susan.* Television: *Norm; Roseanne.* Awards: Obie Award (*Balm in Gilead*); Joseph Jefferson Awards (*Libra, My Thing of Love, Educating Rita, You Can't Take it With You, Coyote Ugly, Balm in Gilead, The Glass Menagerie*); Three Emmy Awards (*Roseanne*). Birthplace: Carbondale, Illinois.

LAURIE METCALF

Ensemble member since 1986. Faculty, Northwestern University Department of Performance Studies since 1970. Steppenwolf: Director: *Valparaiso; Morning Star; Everyman; As I Lay Dying; Earthly Possessions; The Grapes of Wrath* (also Broadway, London, La Jolla); *Born Yesterday; Aunt Dan and Lemon; You Can't Take it With You.* Other Stage including: Broadway: *Seussical; The Visit; Ragtime; The Glass Menagerie;* Lyric Opera of Chicago: *View from the Bridge; Pelleas and Mellisande; La Traviata; Tosca; The Voyage of Edgar Allan Poe;* Goodman Theatre: Associate Director since 1986; *The Government Inspector; She Always Said, Pablo; A Funny Thing Happened on the Way to the Forum; Passion Play; The Winter's Tale; Cry, the Beloved Country; The Good Person of Setyuan; Melanctha;* Chicago Opera Theatre: *The Mother of Us All; The Merry Wives of Windsor; Summer and Smoke; Albert Herring; The Good Soldier Schweik; Four Saints in Three Acts.* Awards: Two Tony Awards (*The Grapes of Wrath*); Three Tony Award nominations (*The Grapes of Wrath* and *Ragtime*); Drama Desk Award and Outer Critics Circle Award (*The Grapes of Wrath*); Joe Callaway Directing Awards (*The Grapes of Wrath* and *Ragtime*), Los Angeles Ovation Award, NAACP Theatre Award and Toronto's Dora Mavor Moore Award (*Ragtime*); Nine Joseph Jefferson Awards; Academy Award nomination for Best Screenplay (*The Accidental Tourist*). Birthplace: Highland Park, Illinois.

FRANK GALATI

MARTHA LAVEY

Ensemble member since 1993. Steppenwolf Artistic Director since 1995. Ph.D. in Performance Studies from Northwestern University. Steppenwolf: *Valparaiso; The Memory of Water; The Designated Mourner; Supple in Combat; Time of My Life; A Clockwork Orange; Talking Heads; Slavs!; Ghost in the Machine; A Summer Remembered; Love Letters; Aunt Dan and Lemon; Savages.* Other Stage including: Goodman, Victory Gardens, Northlight and Remains Theatres. Awards: Sarah Siddons Award; Alumni Merit Award from Northwestern University. Birthplace: Lawrence, Kansas.

GARY SINISE

Co-founder. Steppenwolf Artistic Director 1980 to 1982 and 1985 to 1986. Steppenwolf: Actor: *One Flew Over the Cuckoo's Nest* (also London); *A Streetcar Named Desire; The Grapes of Wrath* (also Broadway, London, La Jolla); *The Caretaker* (also Broadway); *True West* (Off-Broadway); *Streamers* (Kennedy Center); *Loose Ends; Of Mice and Men; Balm in Gilead* (also Off-Broadway); *The Collection; The Caretaker; The 5th of July; Sandbar Flatland; Rosencrantz and Guildenstern Are Dead; Mack, Anything Goes Over the Rainbow; The Indian Wants the Bronx; The Sea Horse.* Director: *Buried Child* (also Broadway); *The Road to Nirvana; Frank's Wild Years; Orphans* (also Off-Broadway, London); *Tracers; The Miss Firecracker Contest; True West* (also Off-Broadway); *Waiting for the Parade; Action.* Film: Director: *Of Mice And Men; Miles from Home.* Actor: *Imposter; Mission to Mars; Reindeer Games; The Green Mile; It's the Rage; Bruno; Snake Eyes; Ransom; Apollo 13; Forrest Gump; Of Mice and Men.* Television: *That Championship Season* (Showtime); *George Wallace* (TNT); *Truman* (HBO); *The Stand.* Awards: Screen Actors Guild Award, Emmy Award and Cable ACE Award *(George Wallace and Truman)*; National Board of Review Award *(Forrest Gump)*; Academy Award nomination *(Forrest Gump)*. Birthplace: Blue Island, Illinois.

BIOGRAPHIES

Ensemble member since 1985. Steppenwolf: *Closer; Side Man; Playland; Death and the Maiden; A Summer Remembered; Love Letters; Cat on a Hot Tin Roof; Bang; Frank's Wild Years; Tracers; And a Nightingale Sang...; Balm in Gilead; Philadelphia, Here I Come!.* Other Stage including: Remains Theatre Ensemble member, productions including *American Buffalo, Speed the Plow*; Victory Gardens Theatre: *Flyovers.* Film: *A Simple Plan; Office Space; I'll Be Home for Christmas; Santa Fe; Gang Related; The Brady Bunch Movie; A Very Brady Sequel; The Gift.* Television: *Fatal Vision; Son of the Morning Star; American Gothic; Midnight Caller; The Babylon Project: Crusade; From the Earth to the Moon* (HBO); *Kiss the Sky* (TMC); *The Switch; When Love Kills; The Practice; Sherman Oaks; Dead Man's Gun - The Photographer* (Showtime) *Outer Limits - Criminal Nature* (Showtime); *Lies He Told; Vital Signs.* Birthplace: Park Ridge, Illinois.

Ensemble member since 1979. Steppenwolf: Actress: *Valparaiso; Side Man* (also Ireland); *The Beauty Queen of Leenane; Picasso at the Lapin Agile* (also Off-Broadway, Los Angeles, San Francisco); *The Rise and Fall of Little Voice* (also Broadway); *Death and the Maiden; Your Home in the West; Earthly Possessions; Another Time; Harvey; The Secret Rapture; Love Letters; The Grapes of Wrath* (also Broadway, London, La Jolla); *Born Yesterday; Little Egypt; Aunt Dan and Lemon; A Lie of the Mind; Cat on a Hot Tin Roof; Bang; Frank's Wild Years; You Can't Take it With You; Miss Julie; The Three Sisters; Stage Struck; Fool for Love; The Hothouse; Cloud 9; The House; Loose Ends; Waiting for the Parade; Arms and the Man; Savages; Absent Friends; Balm in Gilead; Bonjour, La Bonjour.* Director: *Lydie Breeze* (also Australia); *The Common Pursuit; Stepping Out; Ring Round the Moon.* Other Stage including: Arena Stage: *Expecting Isabel*; Arizona Theatre Company: *Who's Afraid of Virginia Woolf?.* Film: *Jungle 2 Jungle; Eye for an Eye; The Astronaut's Wife; Fearless.* Television: *Nothing Sacred; Seinfeld; Home Improvement; Roseanne; The Practice.* Awards: 1991 Sarah Siddons Award *(Another Time)* Birthplace: Dixon, Illinois.

GARY COLE

RONDI REED

RANDALL ARNEY

Ensemble member since 1984. Steppenwolf Artistic Director 1987 to 1995. Geffen Playhouse, Los Angeles, Artistic Director since 2000. Steppenwolf: Director: *The Beauty Queen of Leenane; Picasso at the Lapin Agile* (also Off-Broadway, San Francisco, Los Angeles, England, Japan); *Death and the Maiden; Curse of the Starving Class; Love Letters; The Geography of Luck; A Walk in the Woods; Killers; Bang.* Actor: *Ghost in the Machine; Earthly Possessions; Harvey; Love Letters; The Homecoming; Born Yesterday; A Lie of the Mind; Frank's Wild Years; Lydie Breeze* (also Australia); *You Can't Take it With You; Coyote Ugly* (also Kennedy Center); *Streamers* (Kennedy Center); *Fool for Love; Arms and the Man; Balm in Gilead.* Film: *Mystery, Alaska; The Out of Towners; Chain Reaction.* Television: *Legalese* (TNT); *Weapons of Mass Distraction* (HBO). Birthplace: Effingham, Illinois.

JOHN MALKOVICH

Ensemble member since 1976. Steppenwolf: Actor: *The Libertine; A Slip of the Tongue* (also London); *Burn This* (also Broadway, London, Los Angeles); *True West* (also Off-Broadway); *Of Mice and Men; Big Mother; Death of a Salesman; Say Goodnight, Gracie; Waiting for Lefty; The Glass Menagerie; Philadelphia, Here I Come!; The 5th of July; Our Late Night; Birdbath.* Director: *Hysteria; Libra; The Caretaker* (also Broadway); *Coyote Ugly* (also Kennedy Center); *A Prayer for My Daughter; The House; No Man's Land; Savages; Absent Friends; Balm in Gilead* (also Off-Broadway); *Sandbar Flatland; The Indian Wants the Bronx; The Sea Horse.* Film: Director: *The Dancer Upstairs.* Actor: *Being John Malkovich; The Messenger; Rounders; The Man in the Iron Mask; Con Air; The Ogre; Portrait of a Lady; In the Line of Fire; The Killing Fields; The Sheltering Sky; Places in the Heart; Mulholland Falls; Mary Reilly; Dangerous Liaisons; Of Mice and Men.* Television: *RKO 281* (HBO); *Death of a Salesman.* Awards: Obie Award (*True West*); Emmy Award (*Death of a Salesman*); Academy Award nominations (*In the Line of Fire* and *Places in the Heart*). Birthplace: Benton, Illinois.

B I O G R A P H I E S

Ensemble member since 1985. Steppenwolf: *The Glass Menagerie; Time of My Life; The Mesmerist; Earthly Possessions; Another Time; Love Letters; Reckless; Aunt Dan and Lemon; Cat on a Hot Tin Roof; You Can't Take it With You; Miss Julie; The Three Sisters.* Other Stage including: Broadway: *Stepping Out; The Crucible;* Off-Broadway: *The Seagull; The Two Gentlemen of Verona; Say Goodnight, Gracie;* nine seasons at the Williamstown Theatre Festival; McCarter Theatre; Hartford Stage Company; Philadelphia Drama Guild. Film: *Pollock; Bullets Over Broadway; New York Stories; Radio Days.* Television: *The Sopranos; Law and Order; Cosby; Newhart.* Awards: Joseph Jefferson Award (*Another Time*). Birthplace: Mankato, Minnesota.

Ensemble member since 1983. Steppenwolf: Actor: *One Flew Over the Cuckoo's Nest* (also London); *Side Man* (also Ireland); *The Beauty Queen of Leenane; Morning Star; The Man Who Came to Dinner* (also London); *The Memory of Water; A Streetcar Named Desire; Slaughterhouse-5; Molly Sweeney; Libra; The Road to Nirvana; Ghost in the Machine; Earthly Possessions; Curse of the Starving Class; Love Letters; The Homecoming; A Walk in the Woods; The Grapes of Wrath* (also Broadway, London, La Jolla); *The Common Pursuit; Little Egypt; Bang; Lydie Breeze* (also Australia); *You Can't Take it With You; Stage Struck; The Hothouse; A Moon for the Misbegotten; Balm in Gilead.* Director: *Tavern Story.* Other Stage including: Goodman Theatre: *A Christmas Carol.* Film: *Soul Survivors; U.S. Marshalls; The Net; White Boys.* Television: *Chicago Hope; Missing Persons; Early Edition; Profiler; The Untouchables.* Birthplace: Elmhurst, Illinois.

MOLLY REGAN

RICK SNYDER

TINA LANDAU

Ensemble member since 1997. Steppenwolf: Playwright and Director: *Space* (also Off-Broadway, Mark Taper Forum). Director: *The Berlin Circle; Time to Burn*. Other Stage including: Playwright and Director: Off-Broadway: *Floyd Collins* (also Chicago, Philadelphia, San Diego); *Dream True; Stonewall;* Actors Theatre of Louisville: *1969*. Director: Off-Broadway: *Saturn Returns; Orestes; Trojan Women; Cloud Tectonics* (also La Jolla); *Marisol* (also La Jolla). Film: Screenplay for *Space*. Awards: Princess Grace Award; TCG/NEA Director Fellowship; Pew, J. Alton Jones and Rockefeller Awards. Birthplace: New York, New York.

AUSTIN PENDLETON

Ensemble member since 1987. Steppenwolf: Actor: *Valparaiso; Uncle Bob; Inspecting Carol; Love Letters; Educating Rita* (also Off-Broadway). Director: *Harvey; Cat on a Hot Tin Roof; The Three Sisters; Loose Ends; Say Goodnight, Gracie*. Playwright: *Orson's Shadow; Uncle Bob*. Other Stage including: Actor: Broadway: *The Diary of Anne Frank; Doubles; Hail Strawdyke; Fiddler on the Roof;* Off-Broadway: *Hamlet; Richard III; The Last Sweet Days of Isaac; Oh Dad, Poor Dad, Mamma's Hung You in the Closet and I'm Feelin' So Sad*. Director: Off-Broadway: *The Little Foxes; Spoils of War; The Runner Stumbles;* frequent directing at the Williamstown Theatre Festival. Playwright: *Booth*. Film: *Mr. and Mrs. Bridge; What's Up Doc; Joe the King; The Associate; Trial and Error; Amistad; Sue*. Television: *Homicide; Oz* (HBO); *The Fourth Floor* (HBO); *Liberty* (PBS). Awards: Clarence Derwent Award *(Hail Strawdyke)*; Obie Award *(The Last Sweet Days of Isaac)*. Birthplace: Warren, Ohio.

B I O G R A P H I E S

Ensemble member since 1998. Steppenwolf: *The Glass Menagerie; The Playboy of the Western World* (also Long Wharf Theatre); *The Libertine*. Other Stage including: Off-Broadway: *SubUrbia; Pericles, Prince of Tyre; The Haggadah; Runaways;* Seattle Repertory Theatre: *Uncle Vanya; The Heidi Chronicles; The Sisters Rosensweig; Robbers*. Film: *Backward Looks, Far Corners; 200 Cigarettes; Pecker; Eye of God; Running on Empty; Another Woman; Parenthood; I'm Not Rappaport; I Shot Andy Warhol; Beautiful Girls; Mrs. Parker and the Vicious Circle; Stanley and Iris; Stars and Bars; Shy People; The Mosquito Coast; The Goonies; River Rat*. Television: *ER; The Defenders*. Birthplace: New York, New York.

Ensemble member since 1987. Steppenwolf: *The Infidel; The Man Who Came to Dinner* (also London); *Space; A Fair Country; Slaughterhouse-5; Molly Sweeney; As I Lay Dying; Time of My Life; A Clockwork Orange; Picasso at the Lapin Agile; Inspecting Carol; Awake and Sing!; The Song of Jacob Zulu* (also Broadway, Australia); *A Summer Remembered; Curse of the Starving Class; Harvey; The Geography of Luck; A Walk in the Woods; The Grapes of Wrath* (also Broadway, London, La Jolla); *Killers; Born Yesterday; A Lie of the Mind; Cat on a Hot Tin Roof*. Other Stage including: Broadway: *Death of a Salesman; Carousel;* Goodman Theatre: *Spinning into Butter;* Northlight Theatre: *Belmont Avenue Social Club;* European Repertory Theatre: *Ivanov;* Buckets O'Beckett Festival: *Endgame*. Film: *A Piece of Eden; Love in Action in Chicago; The Crucible; Trial by Jury; The Package*. Television: *Early Edition; NYPD Blue, The Untouchables*. Awards: 1999 William and Eva Fox Foundation Fellowship, Rockefeller Foundation Grant; Joseph Jefferson Award. Birthplace: New Haven, Connecticut.

MARTHA PLIMPTON

ROBERT BREULER

MARIANN MAYBERRY

Ensemble member since 1993. Steppenwolf: *One Flew Over the Cuckoo's Nest* (also London); *Hysteria*; *The Berlin Circle*; *Space*; *A Fair Country*; *Time to Burn*; *The Libertine*; *Everyman*; *As I Lay Dying*; *Time of My Life*; *Slavs!*; *Ghost in the Machine*; *Bite the Hand*; *Tennessee*; *Wrong Turn at Lungfish*; *The Geography of Luck*; *Terry Won't Talk*. Other Stage including: Goodman Theatre: *The Notebooks of Leonardo Da Vinci* (also Off-Broadway); *The Odyssey*; *Mirror of the Invisible World*; Northlight Theater and Alliance Theatre: *How I Learned to Drive*; Lookingglass Theatre: *The Master and Margarita*. Film: *Since You've Been Gone*; *Hole in the Wall*; *Life Sentence*; *Under the Influence*. Birthplace: Springfield, Missouri.

K. TODD FREEMAN

Ensemble member since 1993. Steppenwolf: *One Flew Over the Cuckoo's Nest* (also London); *A Clockwork Orange*; *Libra*; *The Song of Jacob Zulu* (also Broadway, Australia). Other Stage including: Off-Broadway: *Uncle Tom's Cabin*; *Freefall*; *Ubu*; *West Memphis Mojo*; Mark Taper Forum: *Miss Evers' Boys*; *Angels in America*. Film: *The Cider House Rules*; *Grosse Point Blank*; *The End of Violence*; *Grand Canyon*; *House Arrest*; *Eraser*. Television: *NYPD Blue*; *Buffy the Vampire Slayer*; *Sisters*; *A Different World*; *The Killing Mind*. Awards: Tony Award and Outer Critics Circle Award nominations (*The Song of Jacob Zulu*). Birthplace: Houston, Texas.

B I O G R A P H I E S

Ensemble member since 1993. Steppenwolf: *A Streetcar Named Desire*; *My Thing of Love*; *Curse of the Starving Class*; *The Grapes of Wrath* (Broadway). Other Stage including: Broadway: *The Speed of Darkness*; *A Month in the Country*; Off-Broadway: *Down the Shore*. Film: *Stir of Echoes*; *Dream with the Fishes*; *Naked City*; *Entropy*; *What About Bob?*; *D2: The Mighty Ducks*; *Kiss of Death*; *The Addiction*; *Rich in Love*. Television: *Oz* (HBO); *George Wallace* (TNT); *Homicide*; *Breathing Lesson*; *Sherman Oaks*. Awards: Tony Award nomination (*The Speed of Darkness*). Birthplace: Boston, Massachusetts.

Co-founder. Steppenwolf: Director: *One Flew Over the Cuckoo's Nest* (also London); *A Streetcar Named Desire*; *A Clockwork Orange*; *My Thing of Love*; *Reckless*; *Streamers* (Kennedy Center); *Fool for Love*; *And a Nightingale Sang...* (also Off-Broadway); *Of Mice and Men*; *The Lover*. Actor: *Buried Child* (Broadway); *Another Time*; *The Grapes of Wrath* (also Broadway, London, La Jolla); *Orphans* (also Off-Broadway); *Tracers*; *Cloud 9*; *A Prayer for My Daughter*; *The House*; *Loose Ends*; *Action*; *Savages*; *Balm in Gilead* (also Off-Broadway); *Death of a Salesman*; *Waiting for Lefty*; *The Glass Menagerie*; *Exit the King*; *Sandbar Flatland*; *Rosencrantz and Guildenstern Are Dead*; *Our Late Night*; *The Indian Wants the Bronx*. Other Stage including: Director: Off-Broadway: *Eyes for Consuela*; *Brilliant Traces*. Film: *Save the Last Dance*; *House of Mirth*; *The Young Girl and the Monsoon*; *Oxygen*; *Sleepers*; *Fly Away Home*; *The Firm*; *Devil in the Blue Dress*; *No Mercy*. Television: *Oz* (HBO); *That Championship Season* (Showtime); *George Wallace* (TNT); *Thirtysomething*. Awards: Tony Award nomination (*The Grapes of Wrath*); Drama Desk Award nomination (*And a Nightingale Sang...*); Joseph Jefferson Award (*And a Nightingale Sang...*); Cable ACE nomination (*Oz*). Birthplace: Lincoln, Illinois.

KATHRYN ERBE

TERRY KINNEY

JIM TRUE-FROST

Ensemble member since 1989. Steppenwolf: Actor: *The Playboy of the Western World* (also Long Wharf Theatre); *Buried Child* (Broadway); *A Summer Remembered*; *Curse of the Starving Class*; *The Geography of Luck*; *The Homecoming*; *The Grapes of Wrath* (also Broadway, London, La Jolla); *Killers*; *The Common Pursuit*. Director: *The Mesmerist*; *Words and Music*; *Ghost in the Machine*; *Bite the Hand*; *Tennessee*; *Terry Won't Talk*. Other Stage including: Off-Broadway: *Philadelphia, Here I Come!*; Syracuse Stage: *The Beauty Queen of Leenane*; *A Christmas Carol*; Remains Theatre: *Road*; Goodman Theatre: *The Good Person of Szechuan*; *The Iceman Cometh*; Wisdom Bridge Theatre: *Rat in the Skull*. Film: *Affliction*; *Singles*; *The Hudsucker Proxy*; *Far Harbor*. Television: *Two Over Easy* (Showtime). Awards: Joseph Jefferson Award *(Killers)*. Birthplace: Greenwich, Connecticut.

JEFF PERRY

Co-founder. Steppenwolf Artistic Director 1982 to 1985 and 1986 to 1987. Steppenwolf: Actor: *As I Lay Dying*; *Picasso at the Lapin Agile*; *Awake and Sing!*; *The Grapes of Wrath* (also Broadway, London, La Jolla); *A Lie of the Mind*; *You Can't Take it With You*; *The Caretaker* (also Broadway); *Streamers* (Kennedy Center); *The Three Sisters*; *Our Town*; *Cloud 9*; *A Prayer for My Daughter*; *True West*; *Loose Ends*; *Of Mice and Men*; *Arms and the Man*; *No Man's Land*; *Balm in Gilead* (also Off-Broadway); *The Dock Brief*; *Quiet Jeanie Green*; *Death of a Salesman*; *The Collection*; *Waiting for Lefty*; *The Caretaker*; *Exit the King*; *Philadelphia, Here I Come!*; *The 5th of July*; *Sandbar Flatland*; *Rosencrantz and Guildenstern Are Dead*; *Mack, Anything Goes Over the Rainbow*; *The Lover*. Director: *The Homecoming*; *Little Egypt*; *Educating Rita* (also Off-Broadway); *The Hothouse*; *A Moon for the Misbegotten*; *The Loveliest Afternoon of the Year*; *The Lesson*. Film: *Wild Things*; *The Grifters*; *Remember My Name*; *Storyville*; *A Wedding*. Television: Actor: *Nash Bridges*; *My So-Called Life*; *Chicago Hope*; *Into Thin Air*; *Lansky*; *Brooklyn Bridge*; *Thirtysomething*; *Kingfish*. Director: *My So-Called Life*. Birthplace: Highland Park, Illinois.

B I O G R A P H I E S

Ensemble member since 1977. Steppenwolf: *Earthly Possessions*; *Love Letters*; *Reckless*; *Burn This* (also Broadway); *A Lesson from Aloes*; *The Three Sisters*; *The Miss Firecracker Contest*; *Cloud 9*; *And a Nightingale Sang...* (also Off-Broadway); *The House*; *Loose Ends*; *Waiting for the Parade*; *Of Mice and Men*; *Arms and the Man*; *Balm in Gilead*; *Quiet Jeanie Green*; *Bonjour, La Bonjour*; *Say Goodnight, Gracie*; *Waiting for Lefty*; *Exit the King*; *Philadelphia, Here I Come!*; *The 5th of July*; *Our Late Night*. Other Stage including: Broadway: *The Heidi Chronicles*; Off-Broadway: *The Marriage of Bette and Boo*. Film: *The Contender*; *When the Sky Falls*; *It's the Rage*; *The Ice Storm*; *Pleasantville*; *Face-Off*; *The Crucible*; *Nixon*; *Searching for Bobby Fischer*; *Ethan Frome*; *In Country*; *Tucker*; *Peggy Sue Got Married*; *Manhunter*. Television: *Without Warning: The James Brady Story* (HBO); *All My Sons* (PBS); *Evergreen* (NBC miniseries). Awards: Tony Award *(Burn This)*; Obie Award *(The Marriage of Bette and Boo)*; Drama Desk Award, Outer Critics Circle Award, Theatre World Award and Clarence Derwent Award *(And a Nightingale Sang...)*; Tony Award nomination *(The Heidi Chronicles)*; L.A. Film Critics Award and Broadcast Film Critics Award *(Nixon and Pleasantville)*; Golden Globe nomination *(The Crucible)*; Academy Award nominations *(The Crucible and Nixon)*. Birthplace: Rochelle, Illinois.

JOAN ALLEN

Ensemble member since 1979. Steppenwolf: Actor: *The Man Who Came to Dinner* (also London); *Supple in Combat*; *Death and the Maiden*; *The Song of Jacob Zulu*; *Wrong Turn at Lungfish*; *Born Yesterday*; *You Can't Take it With You*; *Orphans* (also Off-Broadway); *Stage Struck*; *Our Town*; *The Hothouse*; *And a Nightingale Sang...*; *A Prayer for My Daughter*; *The House*; *Loose Ends*; *Of Mice and Men*; *Arms and the Man*; *No Man's Land*; *Savages*; *Absent Friends*; *Balm in Gilead*; *Death of a Salesman*; *The Collection*; *Waiting for Lefty*; *Philadelphia, Here I Come!*. Director: *Talking Heads*. Other Stage including: Broadway: *The House of Blue Leaves*; Irish Repertory Theatre: *Long Days Journey into Night*; National Jewish Theatre: *After the Fall*. Film: *She's the One*; *Primal Fear*; *The American President*; *Tin Men*; *Barton Fink*; *The Hudsucker Proxy*; *Moonstruck*; *Say Anything*; *Suspect*. Television: *Frasier*; *Nothing Sacred*. Awards: Tony Award *(The House of Blue Leaves)*; Clarence Derwent Award and Theatre World Award *(Orphans)*; Emmy Award and Golden Globe nominations *(Frasier)*. Birthplace: Manchester, England.

JOHN MAHONEY

GLENNE HEADLY

Ensemble member since 1979. Steppenwolf: *Love Letters; Born Yesterday; Coyote Ugly; The Miss Firecracker Contest; The House; Loose Ends; The Great American Desert; Savages; Absent Friends; Balm in Gilead* (also Off-Broadway); *The Collection; Say Goodnight, Gracie; Waiting for Lefty.* Other Stage including: Broadway: *Arms and the Man;* Off-Broadway: *The Philanthropist; Extremities;* London: *Aunt Dan and Lemon;* Wisdom Bridge Theatre: *Mother Courage;* Goodman Theatre: *Curse of the Starving Class.* Film: *Time Code; Breakfast of Champions; Mr. Holland's Opus; Mortal Thoughts; Dirty Rotten Scoundrels; Dick Tracy; Nadine; 2 Days in the Valley.* Television: *Winchell* (HBO); *And the Band Played On* (HBO); *Bastard Out of Carolina* (Showtime); *My Own Country* (Showtime); *Pronto* (Showtime); *Seize the Day* (PBS); *Lonesome Dove.* Awards: Theatre World Award (*The Philanthropist*); Joseph Jefferson Awards (*Say Goodnight, Gracie; Balm in Gilead; The Miss Firecracker Contest; Coyote Ugly*); Emmy Award nominations (*Lonesome Dove* and *Bastard Out of Carolina*). Birthplace: New London, Connecticut.

FRANCIS GUINAN

Ensemble member since 1979. Steppenwolf: *Mizlansky/Zilinsky or Schmucks; Skylight; The Libertine; The Road to Nirvana; Awake and Sing!; Stepping Out; The Grapes of Wrath* (Broadway); *Little Egypt; A Lesson From Aloes; Coyote Ugly* (also Kennedy Center); *The Miss Firecracker Contest; Cloud 9; And a Nightingale Sang...* (Off-Broadway); *True West; Arms and the Man; No Man's Land; Savages; Absent Friends; Say Goodnight, Gracie; Waiting for Lefty.* Other Stage including: Off-Broadway: *As Is;* Mark Taper Forum: *Space;* Royal George Theatre: *The Nerd;* national tour of *Mass Appeal;* Ivoryton Playhouse: *Sleuth;* Tamarind Theatre: *Black and Blue.* Film: *Guinevere; Apartment Complex; Speed II; Hannibal; Shining Through.* Television: *Star Trek: Voyager; The Practice; Profiler; Nash Bridges; That 70's Show; It's Like... You Know; Law and Order; Eerie, Indiana; The Mighty Jungle; Murder One; George Wallace* (TNT); *Lansky* (HBO); *Any Day Now* (Lifetime). Birthplace: Council Bluffs, Iowa.

B I O G R A P H I E S

Ensemble member since 1979. Steppenwolf: Actor: *Pot Mom; Space* (also Off-Broadway); *My Thing of Love* (also Broadway); *Love Letters; The Homecoming; The Grapes of Wrath* (also London, La Jolla); *Little Egypt; Aunt Dan and Lemon; Cat on a Hot Tin Roof; Frank's Wild Years; Lydie Breeze* (also Australia); *You Can't Take it With You; The Three Sisters; Tracers; The Hothouse; The Miss Firecracker Contest; A Moon for the Misbegotten; And a Nightingale Sang . . .; The House; Loose Ends; No Man's Land; Savages; Balm in Gilead* (also Off-Broadway); *Quiet Jeanie Green; Bonjour, La Bonjour; Waiting for Lefty.* Director: *Your Home in the West; Miss Julie; Stage Struck.* Other Stage including: Actor: Off-Broadway: *New England;* Williamstown Theatre Festival: *Misha's Party;* Northlight Theatre: *The Glass Menagerie.* Director: New Stage: *'night Mother; Long Days Journey into Night;* Free Shakespeare: *Richard II;* Illinois Shakespeare: *King Lear.* Film: *Midnight Run; Mr. Jones; Deceived; Light of Day; In Quiet Night; The Haunting; Men Don't Leave.* Television: *My So-Called Life; My Life and Times; No Greater Love; When Husbands Cheat; The Girl Next Door; A Step Toward Tomorrow; Sandy Bottom Orchestra; Fatal Exposure; Holiday Affair; All Together Now; My Very Best Friend; Innocent Victims; Country Estates; To My Daughter; In the Best Interest of the Child.* Awards: Joseph Jefferson Award (*The Glass Menagerie*). Birthplace: Peoria, Illinois.

Ensemble member since 1976. Steppenwolf: *The Playboy of the Western World; The Road to Nirvana; Curse of the Starving Class; Love Letters; The Homecoming; Little Egypt; Cat on a Hot Tin Roof; Bang; Frank's Wild Years; Lydie Breeze* (also Australia); *Coyote Ugly* (also Kennedy Center); *The Miss Firecracker Contest; A Moon for the Misbegotten; And a Nightingale Sang...* (Off-Broadway); *Waiting for the Parade; Big Mother; Exit the King; Philadelphia, Here I Come!; The 5th of July; Mack, Anything Goes Over the Rainbow; Our Late Night; The Sea Horse; The Lesson.* Other Stage including: Off-Broadway: *Fool for Love.* Film: *Chicago Cab; Breakdown; Three Wishes; Tall Tale; Of Mice and Men.* Television: *Chicken Soup for the Soul* (PAX); *Between Love and Hate; Murder in Green Meadow.* Awards: Chicago Emmy Award (*Murder in Green Meadow*). Birthplace: Pontiac, Illinois.

TOM IRWIN

MOIRA HARRIS

TIM HOPPER

Ensemble member since 1989. Steppenwolf: *The Glass Menagerie*; *Picasso at the Lapin Agile* (also Off-Broadway, Los Angeles); *My Thing of Love*; *Your Home in the West*; *Wrong Turn at Lungfish*; *Love Letters*; *El Salvador*; *Ring Round the Moon*; *The Grapes of Wrath*; *The Common Pursuit*. Other Stage: Broadway: *Present Laughter*; Off-Broadway: *The Dying Gaul*; *More Stately Mansions* (also 1998 Edinburgh Festival and Antwerp's De Singel Theatre). Film: *To Die For*; *Class Action*; *The Last of the Mohicans*; *Ties to Rachel*. Television: *New York Undercover*; *Now and Again*; *Oz* (HBO); *Law and Order*; *Almost Perfect*; *Perfect Murder, Perfect Town* (CBS miniseries). Awards: 1998 Obie Award and 1998 Edinburgh Festival Herald Angel Award (*More Stately Mansions*). Birthplace: Chattanooga, Tennessee.

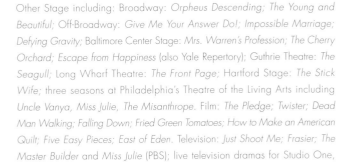

LOIS SMITH

Ensemble member since 1993. Steppenwolf: *Buried Child* (also Broadway); *The Mesmerist*; *The Grapes of Wrath* (also Broadway, London, La Jolla). Other Stage including: Broadway: *Orpheus Descending*; *The Young and Beautiful*; Off-Broadway: *Give Me Your Answer Do!*; *Impossible Marriage*; *Defying Gravity*; Baltimore Center Stage: *Mrs. Warren's Profession*; *The Cherry Orchard*; *Escape from Happiness* (also Yale Repertory); Guthrie Theatre: *The Seagull*; Long Wharf Theatre: *The Front Page*; Hartford Stage: *The Stick Wife*; three seasons at Philadelphia's Theatre of the Living Arts including *Uncle Vanya*, *Miss Julie*, *The Misanthrope*. Film: *The Pledge*; *Twister*; *Dead Man Walking*; *Falling Down*; *Fried Green Tomatoes*; *How to Make an American Quilt*; *Five Easy Pieces*; *East of Eden*. Television: *Just Shoot Me*; *Frasier*; *The Master Builder* and *Miss Julie* (PBS); live television dramas for Studio One, Robert Montgomery Presents and U.S. Steel Hour. Awards: Tony Award nominations (*Buried Child* and *The Grapes of Wrath*); National Society of Film Critics Award (*Five Easy Pieces*). Birthplace: Topeka, Kansas.

B I O G R A P H I E S

Ensemble member since 1984. Steppenwolf: *Earthly Possessions*; *Orphans* (also Off-Broadway, London); *The Three Sisters*; *Our Town*. Other Stage including: Broadway: *Death of a Salesman* (also Goodman Theatre); *Orpheus Descending*; London: *Sunset Boulevard*; Off-Broadway: *The Red Address*; *Brilliant Traces*; *Moonchildren*; Goodman Theatre: *Pal Joey*. Film: *Doe Boy*; *Gregory's Two Girls*; *A Thousand Acres*; *Firelight*; *Eye of God*; *Hoffa*; *Rising Sun*; *About Last Night*; *Liebestraum*; *Sleeping With the Enemy*; *In Country*; *Orphans*; *A Walk on the Moon*; *Miles From Home*. Television: *Nothing Sacred*; *The Hunt for the Unicorn Killer*; *The Wrong Man*; *Orpheus Descending* (TNT). Awards: Outer Critics Circle Award and Drama Desk Award (*Death of a Salesman*); Tony Award nomination (*Death of a Salesman*); Theatre World Award (*Orphans*); Joseph Jefferson Award (*Orphans*); Golden Globe nomination (*Nothing Sacred*). Birthplace: Gurnee, Illinois.

KEVIN ANDERSON

Ensemble member since 1993. Steppenwolf: *Skylight*; *Evelyn and the Polka King*; *Earthly Possessions*; *Harvey*; *The Grapes of Wrath* (Broadway, London, La Jolla); *The Common Pursuit*. Other Stage including: Broadway: *Carousel*; *The Wild Party*; Goodman Theatre; Seattle Repertory Theatre. Film: *Pollock*; *Scent of a Woman*; *Fearless*; *Prelude to a Kiss*; *Charming Billy*. Television: *If These Walls Could Talk* (HBO); *Victim of Love*; *Chicago Hope*; *Dead by Sunset*; American Playhouse; PBS' Great Performances. Birthplace: Chicago, Illinois.

SALLY MURPHY

ERIC SIMONSON

Ensemble member since 1993. Steppenwolf: Director/Adaptor: *Slaughterhouse-5*. Director/Playwright: *Nomathemba (Hope)* (also Kennedy Center). Director: *Slavs!; Evelyn and the Polka King; Inspecting Carol; The Song of Jacob Zulu* (also Broadway, Australia); *The Secret Rapture*. Actor: *The Grapes of Wrath* (also Broadway, London, La Jolla). Other Stage including: Playwright/Director: Milwaukee Repertory Theatre: *Worksong*. Adaptor/Director: Huntington Theatre: *The Last Hurrah; Bang the Drum Slowly* (also Next Theatre). Director: Minnesota Opera: *La Boheme; Bokchoy Variations; The Magic Flute;* Next Theatre: *Knuckle; Coriolanus; The Normal Heart;* Court Theatre: *Othello;* Huntington Theatre: *Hamlet*. Film: Director: *Hamlet* (co-directed with Campbell Scott); *On Tip Toe; Topa Topa Bluffs; Ladies Room L.A.* Television: Actor: *Seinfeld; The Ben Stiller Show; The Untouchables*. Awards: Princess Grace Award; NCCJ Award; Tony Award nomination *(The Song of Jacob Zulu)*. Birthplace: Milwaukee, Wisconsin.

B I O G R A P H I E S

RICHARD CHRISTIANSEN is senior writer and chief critic for the *Chicago Tribune*. A veteran Chicago arts observer and an award-winning writer and editor, he covers a variety of subjects, including contemporary art, theater, dance and film. Christiansen began his career as a general assignment reporter for the *City News Bureau* in 1956 and was later hired by the *Chicago Daily News* as a general assignment reporter and, eventually, critic-at-large. In 1978, he came to the *Chicago Tribune*, serving as critic-at-large and then entertainment editor. He has received the Chicago Newspaper Guild's Service to Journalism Award, the Marshall Field Award for Excellence in Editorial Work and a 1982 Tribune Outstanding Professional Performance Award. Christiansen is a member of the board of directors of The Three Arts Club of Chicago and chairman of the club's literary committee. In 1993, he received the first annual Beatrice Spachner Award of the Auditorium Theatre Council for his contributions to the arts in Chicago. In 1997, he received a special Joseph Jefferson Award for his contributions to Chicago theater. Christiansen is seven times a member of the Pulitzer Prize drama jury, twice as its chairman. In 1998, he was inducted into the Chicago Journalism Hall of Fame.

DON DELILLO has written eleven novels and two stage plays. He was awarded the Jerusalem Prize in 1999, the first American to be so honored. His last novel, *Underworld*, won the Howells Medal of the American Academy of Arts and Letters.

SAM SHEPARD has written forty-five plays, including *Buried Child, Fool For Love, True West* and *A Lie of the Mind*. In 1979 he was awarded the Pulitzer Prize for Drama for *Buried Child*. His screenplay for *Paris, Texas* won the Golden Palm Award at the 1984 Cannes Film Festival. Eleven of his plays have received Obie Awards. In 1986, he was elected to the American Academy of Arts and Letters, and in 1992, he received the Gold Medal for Drama from the Academy. In 1994, he was inducted into the Theatre Hall of Fame. An actor as well as a writer, he has appeared in numerous plays and films, and received an Academy Award nomination for his performance in *The Right Stuff*.

KURT VONNEGUT was born November 11, 1922, in Indianapolis, Indiana, the son and grandson of Indianapolis architects. He is the author of twelve novels, two short story collections, two collections of essays and one play. He is a member of the American Academy of Arts and Letters, and the honorary president of the American Humanist Association. He has a master's degree in anthropology from the University of Chicago, was a former reporter for the *Chicago City News Bureau*, and has taught creative writing at the University of Iowa, Harvard University, and the City College of New York. He is married, the father of seven children, four of them adopted, and presently lives in Northampton, Massachusetts.

TERRY JOHNSON's work as a writer includes: *Dead Funny* which opened at the Hampstead Theatre and enjoyed two successful West End runs at the Vaudeville and Savoy Theatres, and *Hysteria*, at the Duke of Yorks Theatre. Work for the Royal National Theatre includes his adaptation of Edward Ravenscroft's *The London Cuckolds,* and the stage version of *Cor, Blimey!* (entitled *Cleo, Camping, Emmanuelle and Dick*) which won the Olivier Award for Best Comedy. Recent work as a director includes Shelagh Stephenson's *The Memory of Water* (Vaudeville Theatre), David Farr's *Elton John's Glasses* (Queen's Theatre) and Philip Ridley's *Sparkelshark* for the Royal National Theatre. In 1996, he directed the American premiere of Stephen Jeffreys' *The Libertine,* starring John Malkovich. For television he directed his own *Cor Blimey!* and Tim Firth's *Neville's Island,* contributed two dramas: *Blood and Water* and *The Chemistry Lesson* to the BBC Ghosts season and wrote *The Bite* for BBC/ABC Australia. His screenplay of *Insignificance* was directed by Nicolas Roeg and was the official British Entry at Cannes in 1985. He has recently directed Kathleen Turner in the world stage premiere of *The Graduate.*

CHARLES L. MEE has had two pieces produced at Steppenwolf, *Time to Burn* and *The Berlin Circle,* both directed by Tina Landau. Among his more recent work, *Summertime* was recently produced at the Magic Theatre in San Francisco and *Big Love* performed at the Humana Festival of 2000 at the Actors Theatre of Louisville where it was directed by Les Waters, and it will perform, too, at the Berkeley Repertory Theatre in San Francisco, at the Long Wharf Theatre in New Haven, Connecticut, at the Goodman Theatre in Chicago, and, finally, as part of the Next Wave Festival at the Brooklyn Academy of Music. His work is made possible by the support of Richard B. Fisher and Jeanne Donovan Fisher.

MICHAEL BROSILOW has been Steppenwolf Theatre Company's resident photographer since 1987. Based in Chicago, Mr. Brosilow's work includes theater, studio and commercial photography. His work has been seen in national and international magazines, newspapers and publications. Mr. Brosilow is a graduate of the University of Illinois, Chicago.

LISA EBRIGHT is a Chicago-based photographer whose various credits include stage, screen, commercial and studio work as well as teaching and lecturing. Her work has appeared in national magazines and newspapers and she has exhibited her work nationally and internationally. Ms. Ebright was Steppenwolf's resident photographer from 1976 to 1986. She is a graduate of Barat College and a member of the American Society of Media Photographers.

KEVIN RIGDON designed over 100 productions as resident designer for Steppenwolf Theatre Company from its inception in 1974 through 1997, and took numerous photographs of the company's early work. His lighting and scenic designs include Broadway, Off-Broadway, national and international theater work. Mr. Rigdon has received two American Theatre Wing Design Awards, a Drama-louge Award and seven Joseph Jefferson Awards. He has also been nominated for two Tony Awards and three Drama Desk Awards. Mr. Rigdon is the associate director/design of the Alley Theatre and teaches design at the University of Houston.

ACCOLADES

PRODUCER

Timothy J. Evans

ASSOCIATE PRODUCER

Apphia H. Parsons

PORTRAITS & BOOK DESIGN

Victor Skrebneski

DESIGN/PRODUCTION DIRECTION

Gregory Scott Vallarta

GRATEFUL ACKNOWLEDGMENTS

Jennifer Bielstein

Michael Brosilow

Jeff Caso

Richard Christiansen

Don DeLillo

Lisa Ebright

Robert Englebright

Michael Gennaro

Terry Johnson

Donna La Pietra

Marshall Field's

Charles L. Mee

Dennis Minkel

Jovanna Papadakis

Dominique Raccah

Kevin Rigdon

Phyllis Schuringa

Sam Shepard

Judith Simons

Michele Volansky

Kurt Vonnegut

To my thirty-five new and astonishing pals... Thank you

Thank you Thank you Thank you Thank you Thank you

Thank you Thank you Thank you Thank you Thank you

Thank you Thank you Thank you Thank you Thank you

Thank you Thank you Thank you Thank you Thank you

Thank you Thank you Thank you Thank you Thank you

Thank you Thank you Thank you Thank you Thank you

Thank you Thank you Thank you Thank you, for all of the

joy and love that you give to the world and to me. Victor

STEPPENWOLF

AT TWENTY-FIVE

PORTRAITS BY
VICTOR SKREBNESKI

This book was made possible by a generous and deeply appreciated gift from Marshall Field's.

Marshall Field's is the Presenting Sponsor of Steppenwolf Theatre Company's 25th Anniversary Season.

"And It All Happened in the Theater" by Richard Christiansen. Copyright © 2000 by Richard Christiansen.
"Finding the Dark Heart" by Don DeLillo. Copyright © 2000 by Don DeLillo.
"Guts" by Sam Shepard. Copyright © 2000 by Sam Shepard.
"You Can Go Home Again" by Kurt Vonnegut. Copyright © 2000 by Kurt Vonnegut.
"The Libertine, 1996" by Terry Johnson. Copyright © 2000 by Terry Johnson.
"Risks" by Charles L. Mee. Copyright © 2000 by Charles L. Mee.

Portrait Reproduction Copyright © 2000 Victor Skrebneski.

Published by Sourcebooks, Inc.
P. O. Box 4410, Naperville, Illinois 60567-4410
(630) 961-3900
FAX: (630) 961-2168

Skrebneski, Victor,
   Steppenwolf at 25 ; a photographic celebration of an actor's theater /portraits by Victor Skrebneski ; production photographs by Michael Brosilow, Lisa Ebright, Kevin Rigdon.
     p. cm.
   ISBN 1-57071-583-1 (alk. paper)
   1. Steppenwolf Theatre Company – Pictorial works. 2. Steppenwolf Theatre Company – History. I. Title: Steppenwolf at twenty-five. II. Title.

PN2277.C42 S455 2000
792'.09773'11–DC21

                                                                          00-057366

Printed and bound in the United States of America
First printing, October 2000